Programs for
Financial Calculations

By the same author

Financial Calculations for Business
The Sinclair Book of Management Calculations
The Martin Book of Management Calculations

Available direct from the author:

UK Securities, Loans and Banking Calculations Book
(and programs related to the HP 67 & 97
programmable calculators)
Solutions Handbook Fixed Interest Loans (related to
the HP-12C programmable calculator)

PROGRAMS FOR FINANCIAL CALCULATIONS

A SOLUTIONS BOOK FOR THE HEWLETT
PACKARD 17B & 19b BUSINESS CALCULATORS

CHRISTIAN de LISLE

KOGAN
PAGE

*While every effort has been made to ensure the accuracy of
the information contained in this book, it should be used for
guidance only. The author does not accept responsibility for
any loss or damage suffered by readers as a result of any error
or omission in formulae, calculations, tables or descriptive text.*

First published in Great Britain in 1989 by
Kogan Page Limited,
120 Pentonville Road, London N1 9JN

British Library Cataloguing in Publication Data

de Lisle, Christian
    Programs for financial calculations.
    1. Business firms. Financial management.
    Calculations. Use of pocket electronic
    calculators
    I. Title
    658.1'5'02854
    ISBN 1-85091-835-X

Printed and bound in Great Britain by
Biddles Ltd, Guildford and King's Lynn

Contents

Chapter 10   The UK Market and Anomaly Bonds

Chapter 11   Bills, Certificates of Deposit, Notes etc

Acknowledgements

It would be discourteous if I did not thank Waterlow Publishing for their kindness in allowing me to reproduce some sections, tables and the like from my book *Business Interest Calculations*, published by them several years ago.   I am indeed most grateful.

My thanks are also due to all those in Kogan Page who have helped with advice and encouragement in the production of this small manual. As is well known, the production of such a book, unlike that of a novel, is fraught with the possibility of an attack by gremlins whose aim it is to mix up the mathematical signs and confuse the reader. Every effort has been made to combat them but should any reader find a sign missing or figures transposed, the author would greatly appreciate a note pointing out the error.

Financial markets are never static so should readers know of any late night changes in format or "rules" such information would, again, be most gratefully received. And hopefully the next edition of this manual will be greatly enhanced!

The printed word . . .
In view of the recent interest in desk-top publishing a comment on the typesetting of this manual may not come amiss. The font employed is Times Roman (11 pt) which reverts to mono spacing for the formulae, tables, shaded menu calculations etc.

The lay out and general format was entirely the author's responsibility, the text being word-processed on PC Write, using an HP Vectra and laser printer. The pages were then photographed; consequently any errors cannot be blamed on my friends at Kogan Page!

Lastly, my thanks to Tony Collinson of HP, a friend of many years standing, for checking the programs and calculations.

C. de L. January 1989.

Introduction

The *Owner's Manuals* and other HP-related *Solution Books* provide a variety of excellent programs, but many are, not unnaturally, US-orientated. Some of the programs provided in the following pages attempt to redress the balance.

The written-in formulae

When inspecting some of the formulae/programs in this book the term "SGN", as for example in SGN(N), or a value such as (XT-XT) may sometimes be seen. Such values have no mathematical significance in the equations and can, if wished, be disregarded. Their purpose is merely to rearrange the order in which the menu boxes, or labels, appear in the program. For the order of appearance in the menu display follows the order of alpha references written into the formula and it may well be that in some cases a different menu format will be considered more suitable.

Sometimes the name of the program to be keyed-in is followed by stars * *. This denotes that there are two quite separate programs within one program cover. If the values within these two programs are not shared all values are available. But if some of the values are shared then some of the less important values may not always be available.

The keyboard - the BOXES and [INPUT]

The menu boxes are printed on a shaded background where they occur in the course of calculations, but if referred to in the main text are shown in [CAPITALS].

Keystrokes are shown in brackets thus: [INPUT] or [EXIT]. Signs for plus, minus, equals etc are also bracketed as [+], [−] and [=] when part of a keystroke discipline. The yellow SHIFT key is represented by ▌ as in ▌[LAST]. The data values to be input are shown below the corresponding boxes and can be input in any order, unless otherwise specified, except that the answer required, represented by the box with a question mark (?) underneath, must be pressed *last*.

Should the user wish to input into a box a value which is on display, having previously been calculated, he must press [INPUT] first, for if this is not done the calculator will simply re-calculate the previous answer derived from the previous data – and the display value will be lost!

All the calculations, unless otherwise stated, are worked through to the full 12-digit precision of the business calculators. Should the reader therefore pick up an example in the middle, without starting at the beginning of the explanation, there may possibly be a slight decimal difference owing to payments being rounded, etc.

All examples quoted can of course be applied to any decimal currency but some mental adjustments may sometimes be needed; a home loan to a value of, say, 50,000 in dollars or sterling may be considered reasonable in either the UK or the States but the same number of lira, in Italy, might perhaps just purchase a superior rabbit hutch!

The HP-17B and the HP-19B
Apart from the fact that the HP-19B, unlike the HP-17, is both a financial *and* a scientific unit, there are also one or two minor keying-in differences between the two units which are naturally outlined in the respective *Manuals*. There are also a few minor differences in the programming methods.

While some 19B keyed-in programs, because of the extra scientific facilities, cannot be transported to the HP-17B, any programs designed for the HP-17B can be employed on the HP-19B. Consequently in the following pages all programs relate to the HP-17B. HP-19B users should have no difficulty in making any necessary adjustments.

Rounding values to £/p, $/c, etc
In business and commerce when calculations are undertaken, which relate to actual payments, as opposed to theoretical payments, it is essential, if further calculations are to continue, to round the payments to their *cash* value. For no borrower is likely to repay (say) £10.5123456 monthly. He will, of course, repay £10.51 or, if the lender so requires, £10.52

Consequently many examples in this book require rounding to 2 places of decimals in the middle of the calculations.

Unhappily, life sometimes is full of surprises; whereas, like all other HP calculators, the HP-19B has a rounding key (admittedly buried in the [MATH] mode) the HP-17B has not. This is particularly unfortunate, for whereas the HP-19B has a four-line display the HP-17B has only a one-liner. Consequently rounding has to be done manually and it is often necesssary to jot down the values concerned on a scratch pad.

To obviate this irritation, I use a few program keystrokes which can be kept at the top of the list of programs or written just above or below any program continually in use.

Key in:

$$RND(VALUE:FIX)=RND$$

VALUE   FIX   RND

For example, round the following: 1.11111111111 and 12,345.346789, both to 2, 3, and 6 decimal places.

First prepare the calculator to [DSP] ALL :

VALUE	FIX	RND	
1.11111111111	2	?	= 1.11
	3	?	= 1.111
	6	?	= 1.111111

VALUE	FIX	RND	
12,345.3456789	2	?	= 12,345.35
	3	?	= 12,345.346
	6	?	= 12,345.345679

However, several programs provided in this book have [FIX] built into program menu to save time and trouble.

When using such programs it is important always to check the fix value every time a new calculation is commmenced for, if a fix has been previously used in another (shared) program, the fix register will be in accordance with the last fix employed. Also, when program values are cleared the fix defaults to 0.

Rounding is imperative in all calculations where payments are made in practice, but the converse is true of theoretical calculations. The value of the fix facility lies in the fact that sometimes the statistician may want see the full precision value of a particular calculation which would be impossible if the rounding discipline, to 2 places of decimals, was written into the program.

Furthermore, the rounding of the payments may affect the precision of subsequent calculations. In the event of further calculations being required, unrelated to the rounded payments, recalculate the payments at [FIX] 11 (the maximum permissible) before undertaking that part of the calculation.

CHAPTER 1

Percentages and Conversions

The UK Consumer Credit Act (1974)

As the above Act conditions much of UK lending calculations, and in some cases the actual rates offered, it may be useful to consider the regulations straight away. The Consumer Credit Act (1974) and the disclosure regulations are somewhat complex; for not every loan or leasing requires disclosure. Nevertheless many firms now disclose in all circumstances, either from social conscience or to be on the safe side. The (UK) Office of Fair Trading (OFT) provides various pamphlets, etc related to the regulations.

In brief, any "loan" (which includes leasing) from May 1985 if below £15,000 (and all loans where the collateral is based on land or "property") requires the disclosure of the term of the loan, the Annual Percentage Rate of charge (usually shortened to APR), and the Total Amount Payable (TAP). The TAP is the total amount of payments made *plus* any extra fees, balloon payments etc, relating to the loan in question. The Total Charge for Credit (the TCC), if required, is the TAP *less* the original capital (loan) amount.

The British and American APR

In Britain the APR is the effective rate of interest, as opposed to the nominal rate, *truncated* (*not* rounded) to one place of decimals. Unhappily, APR in the United States refers to the nominal rate, not the effective, and as the Hewlett-Packard *Manuals* are US-orientated it must remembered that wherever they mention the APR it is the nominal rate and *not* the effective rate of interest that is being referred to. In the pages below the APR refers to the UK APR – where there is any room for doubt (US)APR or (UK)APR will be used.

Conversions

To find the effective rate which, when truncated, provides the APR, first calculate the periodic rate, and hence the nominal rate, from which the efffective rate can be determined.

To convert a given nominal rate to the effective one:

$$100 \left[\left(1 + \frac{NOM}{100 \times p} \right)^p - 1 \right] = \text{Effective rate \%}$$

Where p = the number of compounding periods in any one year
(e.g., 12 monthly, 4 quarterly or 2 semi-annual)

Thus 10% nominal with monthly "rests" converts to:

$$100 \left[\left(1 + \frac{10}{100 \times 12} \right)^{12} - 1 \right] = 10.471307\% \ Eff\%$$

```
10 [÷] 1200 [+] 1 [yˣ] 12 [–] 1 [x] 100   = 10.471307   Eff%
                                          = 10.4         APR%
```

▌ [MAIN]

FIN	ICNV	PER	=	NOM%	EFF%	P
				10	?	12	= 10.471307 Eff%

To (re)convert an effective rate to its nominal merely reverse the above formula:

$$(100 \times p) \times \left[\left(1 + \frac{EFF}{100} \right)^{1/p} - 1 \right] = \text{Nominal \%}$$

```
10.471307 [÷] 100 [+] 1 [yˣ] 12 [1/x] [–] 1 x 1200 = 10.00
```

When the compounding periods differ from the payments periods

The tip is to calculate the effective rate of the interest and then, using that value, to find its nominal rate from the payment structure.

For example, Canadian mortgages are usually calculated by assuming that interest is charged semi-annually but repayments are required monthly. If the quoted rate is 11% nominal what is the "working" rate?

Convert the interest of 11% nominal to its effective rate, employing the *interest* rests namely semi-annually (2), and then reconvert this effective to its nominal using the *payment* rests, namely monthly (12).

NOM%	EFF%	P
11	?	2
	= 11.302500	
?		12
= 10.756073		

As can be seen, the effective rate is, correctly, the same for both the semi-annual conversion and the monthly conversion, namely 11.30%. See the keyed-in program for FLAT/NOM/EFF below, where the above calculation is again used as an example.

Nominal rate converted to continuous effective rate

The box menu [FIN] [ICNV] [CONT] will provide the in-built HP continuous compounding program displaying [NOM%] [EFF%] An input of 10 to [NOM%] and pressing [EFF%] gives 10.517092. This value can equally well be found by:

(17B) 10 [÷] 100 ▌ [MATH]   EXP [−] 1 [x] 100 [=] 10.517092
(19B) 10 [÷] 100 ▌ [MATH] LOGS EXP [−] 1 [x] 100 [=] 10.517092

Simple interest calculations

Let us assume that a lender provides a short-term bridging loan for the selling of one house and the purchasing of another. Since this is a property transaction, disclosure will be required. Assuming the loan is for £10,000 at 15% simple interest for 18 days, what is the the APR and the TAP?

£10,000 at 15% = £1,500.00 and 1,500/365 x 18 = 74.00 interest. The total amount paid, the TAP, is therefore £10,074.00

The APR, the truncated effective rate, cannot be found from the above 15% rate for that rate is a simple interest rate, and the effective must be taken from a true rate for the APR disclosure. As a rough test, the effective is usually approximately double the simple rate.

The first thing is to find the payments over the 18 days:
10,074 [÷] 18 [=] 559.666667 and so using the HP program:

```
▌ [MAIN]  FIN    TVM
     N     I%YR   PV     PMT    FV    OTHER  365  P/YR  [EXIT]
     18    ?    −10000  559.67  0
           = 28.392081 NOMINAL rate%
```

Flat rates to APR%

Whereas simple interest, or flat rate, quotations are quite normal in the USA they are used less in the UK than they used to be. For if a UK lender is legally bound to reveal the APR it means that he will have previously needed to calculate the true nominal and effective rates of interest – and if you know the true nominal rate why not quote it? In the States, incidentally, the simple interest rate is called the "add-on" rate, implying that something has to be added to find the true rate – as indeed it has.

For those who deal with such matters as a matter of routine, and who need to calculate the APR from flat rates on a daily basis, the program below may be useful.

Assume a £5,000 loan over 3 years, with required monthly payments, with a simple interest rate quotation of 10% (flat). What are the monthly payments, the true nominal interest rate and the APR? 10% of £5,000 is £500 for one year; as the loan is for 3 years the total amount to be repaid is therefore £5,000 + (500 x 3) which equals £6,500. To discover the 36 monthly payments required: £6,500/36 = £180.56 (rounded to actual payments).

Key in the following **FLAT/NOM/EFF * *** program:

FLAT/NOM/EFF:IF(S(FLAT%) OR S(TRUE%):((IN V(FLAT%xYEARS÷100+1))xSGN(TRUE%)xYEARSxP) −USPV(TRUE%÷P:YEARSxP):((SPFV(NOM%÷P:P)−1)x100)−EFF%)

(Ensure a space before/after OR above)
FLAT% YEARS TRUE%   P   NOM%   EFF%

So taking the above example:

FLAT%	YEARS	TRUE%	P			NOM%	EFF%
10	3	?	12				
		=17.92		[INPUT] press		?	= 19.46 (EFF)
		[STO 0]					= 19.4 (APR)

The [INPUT] must be pressed when switching programs. The [P] factor is common to both programs.

```
[RCL] TRUE% [STO 0] ▌ MAIN  FIN   TVM  OTHER 12 P/YR END MODE
is on display — if not adjust as required.[EXIT]
   N      I%YR   PV     PMT    FV    OTHER
   36   [RCL0]  -5000    ?      0
                       = 180.56 (The quoted rate checks)
```

Assume the flat rate was 16.75%, over a term of 5 years, with monthly payments required. What is the nominal rate and the APR?

```
▌ MAIN  SOLVE  ↑↓  FLAT/NOM/EFF  CALC
FLAT%  YEARS  TRUE%    P         NOM%  EFF%
16.75    5      ?      12
                =27.15      [INPUT] press   ?  = 30.80 (EFF)
                               ▌ [SHOW]        = 30.796630118
                                               = 30.7 (APR)
```

Nom/Eff

This program can be used quite separately from the simple interest rate finding program, as instanced by the Canadian mortgage calculation above, where we had a 11% nominal rate and where the payments were made monthly but the compounding for interest was semi–annual. To find the effective rate:

FLAT%	YEARS	TRUE%	P	NOM%	EFF%		
			2	11	?		= 11.302500
			12	?			= 10.756073

Reverting to the simple interest calculations example above, where we had a 15% simple interest rate for an 18 day bridging loan:

```
FLAT%  YEARS  TRUE%    P
 15    18÷365   ?      365                    NOM%   EFF%
              =28.36         [INPUT] press      ?   = 32.77
```

Simple interest additional periods

When interest is added each period, month by month or year by year, it is almost always calculated by compound interest. When, then, would the additional period interest be at simple interest?

A good example is the 1988 National Savings "Yearly Plan" in which, according to the prospectus, monthly deposits are made only during year 1 and, providing the certificate is held for a further 4 years, the full 5-year tax-free return is stated to be precisely 7%. To effect these parameters the accruing interest over the first 12 months had to be at *simple* interest at a rate of rate of 5.25%. The remaining four years being at 7.25% at annual compound interest.

Employing a schedule for a £100 monthly deposit, each month being at 5.25% simple interest, will find a value at the end of the year of £1,234.68, and $1,234.68 \times (1 + 7.25/100)^4 = 1,633.59$

The schedule would look like this:

```
£100               x (1 + (5.25/1200)) = 100.4375
(100.4375 + 100)   x      1.004375     = 201.3144
(201.3144 + 100)   x         "         = 302.6327  and so on...
```

Is there not an easier method of finding the end value without making a schedule?

A useful tip is to "average the term", in this case $1+2+3+4 \ldots$
$+ 12 = 78$ and $78/12 = 6.5$. The rate multiplied by this factor
will be *almost* correct. The "average" can be achieved by
$(12 + 1)/2 = 6.5$ Using this method the value of the
investor's savings at the end of the first year is:

```
(((Term + 1) ÷ 2 x Rate ÷ 100 ÷  P)+1) x Deposit x Term =  Value
((( 12  + 1) ÷ 2 x 5.25 ÷ 100 ÷ 12)+1) x   100   x  12    = £1,234.13
                    against the schedule value (above) of   £1,234.68
```

This algorithm, if copied exactly, provides a program if
required.

The above tip can be checked by calculating a schedule of the
same parameters over a term of 6 months which will provide a
value of £609.25, near enough to the result obtained when
calculated by algorithm:

```
(1 + (((6 + 1)/2 x 5.25)/1200)) x 600 = £609.1875
```

Taking a further example, assume $50 is being deposited each
month for 3 months at 10% simple interest. A schedule
produces:

```
 50.00 x (1 + 10/1200) =
 50.00 x    1.00833    =  50.42 + 50
100.42 x       "       = 101.25 + 50
151.25 x       "       = 152.51        = $152.51
```

Whereas the algorithm yields:

```
(1 + (((3 + 1)/2 x 10.0)/1200))  x 150 = $152.50
```

and over a whole year:

```
(1 + (((12 + 1)/2 x 10.0)/1200)) x 600 = $632.50
as against a schedule value of          $633.51
```

It will be seen, therefore, that although the algorithm method
is not precise it is sufficiently accurate for most requirements –
and is an extremely useful check on a schedule if such a
method has, in the end, to be employed.

The sum of percentages.

In January 1989, in the UK, a Government National Savings bond, known as the Lawson Bond — after the then Chancellor of the Exchequer — was issued. The terms were that if the bond was held for five years the gross return would be 12% and the net return, for those paying tax at the basic rate of 25%, would be 9.012%.

These rates were achieved by rating the bond at 5.50% for the first year, 8.50% in the second year, 11.50% in the third year, 14.50% in the fourth year, and 20.60% in the fifth and final year — the rolled up income being subject to tax *each year*, which slightly took the gilt off the ginger bread!

$$((1.0550 \times 1.0850 \times 1.1150 \times 1.1450 \times 1.2060)^{1/5}) -1, \times 100 = 12.00\%$$

And as tax had to be paid each year on notional income (!), the percentages have to be brought to net by 5.50% x .75 = 4.125% which divided by 100 plus 1 = 1.041250:

$$((1.041250 \times 1.063750 \times 1.086250 \times 1.108750 \times 1.15450)^{1/5})$$
$$-1, \times 100 = 9.021\%$$
$$(net)$$

From the above it will be seen that the gross return is *not* the five annual rates added, and then divided by 5, to show 12.12%

But it is easy to make mistakes when percentages have to be added or subtracted.

For example. adding 15% + 20% + 10% – 4% is *not* 41% but:

$$(1.15 \times 1.20 \times 1.10 \div 1.04) - 1, \times 100 = 45.96\%$$

Another common misconception is to suppose that if inflation is running at, say, 20% p.a. and if the current lending rate is 10% the return is a negative 10%. In fact, the true return is:

$$(1.10/1.20) - 1, \times 100 = -8.33\%$$

And, incidentally, with a simple interest profile, 10% – 10% is *not* zero! In fact, it is – 1% and the keystrokes below will prove the point, which some disbelieve!

$$100 \ [+] \ 10 \ [\%] \ [-] \ 10 \ [\%] \ [-] \ 100 \ [=] \ -1\%$$

Some percentage reminders
Even in the best circles percentages are sometimes wrongly calculated, banks have been known to make mistakes – and so have politcal parties!

During one British election, the manifestos of two of the political parties stated categorically that if inflation continued unchecked at 20% annually, a £100 would be only worth £85 the following year. Which is mathematical nonsense!

True, £100 less 15 percent is 100 x (1 – .15) = £85.00 if you are working according to a simple interest discounting process, but if, for example, you are deducting VAT (at 15%) from a purchase to find the gross value you would be wrong to calculate by this method.

The gross value of a purchase costing £86.96 plus VAT is:

$$£86.96 \times 1.15 = £100.00$$

consequently the true gross value of £100 less VAT at 15% must be:

$$£100 \div 1.15 = £86.96$$
$$\text{NOT} \quad £100 \times (1 - .15) = £85.00$$

Thus, we should always be absolutely clear , for any particular problem, exactly which type of percentage is required; and politicians, perhaps, could do well to remember this when discussing inflation!

Sometimes it is necessary to find the VAT amount from a given [value + VAT]: in that case the simplest method is to divide by the "useful factor" of 1.15/.15 = 7.66667:

```
£100 ÷ 7.66666 = 13.043478
Check              13.043478/.15 = 86.956522 and x 1.15 = 100.00
```

When considering annual percentages against periodic rates, another error is, unhappily, very prevalent; for many people seem to think that 12% per annum is 1% monthly. The *effective* rate of 1% monthly is 12.65% and *not* 12%.

The keystrokes are:

```
1.00 [÷] 100 [+] 1 [^] 12 [–] 1 [x] 100 [=] 12.68%
```

The UK "Composite Rate"

Years ago, when the Government first instructed building societies to pay interest to their depositors net of tax and, at each year end, to remit to the Revenue the tax value of all the interest due to their depositors, the building societies argued that such a demand was grossly unfair and unrealistic.   For, they pointed out, many of their investors were non-tax payers.

In the event, it was agreed that only a "composite rate of tax" (CRT) need be remitted.   The CRT stood for many years at 25.25% against a basic income tax rate of 30%.   At the beginning of 1989 the CRT was adjusted to 23.25% related to the then basic rate of 25%.

For many years, with the advent of the CRT, building societies paid their investors net, whereas banks paid gross;   and a bewildering plethora of rates, provided by various competing building societies and institutions, appeared in advertisments aimed at inducing the public to invest.

In 1985 the Government produced legislation whereby interest on all loans, with a few minor technical exceptions, would be paid to investors net of tax.   One of the results was that a major problem arose, namely how should the institutions advise their clients of the true effective rate of their loans.

For example, in the old days, if the interest on a loan was paid monthly at 10% gross the effective rate was well known to be 10.47%. But if the tax rate was, say, 25% the advertised net rate is 10 x .75 = 7.50% What then is the effective rate?

Some banks, happily, advertised the effective rate, as 10.47% (UK APR 10.4%), grossing up the net rate to its gross nominal *before* converting to the effective. Others, more correctly, advertised as 10.35% (UK APR 10.3%) converting the net rate to its effective and *then* grossing up. The subsequent confusion was so great that the Bank of England had to step in and rule that the calculation would be as follows:

```
10% at 25% basic tax rate is 10 x.75 =  7.50% net nominal
```

$$100 \times ((1 + 7.50/1200)^{12}) - 1) = 10.35\% \text{ gross effective}$$

The "rule" being to convert the net rate to its effective, *before* converting to the gross profile.

Vulgar fractions
It is simple to convert a vulgar fraction to a decimal, 10 and 5/8th becomes 10.625, but, perhaps, not so easy to reverse the process. The prices of stocks and bonds are often quoted in vulgar fraction form and such a requirement can be an irritation, especially if one is in a hurry.

There is no simple way of finding the "nearest to the true" and it becomes a matter of trial and error. The program below may be of use to those who deal constantly with such conversions as a matter of routine.

The method is to multiply the decimal fraction by different base values, say, 8, 16, 32, or even 64 until the resulting rounded integer is an *un*even number (apart from 1, except very occasionally). Divide this uneven number by the base and the answer is a vulgar fraction. If the result does not appear sufficiently close to the given requirement, double the base value and try again.

For example a price found as 96.1875 could be converted to a vulgar fraction as follows:

```
.1875 x  8 = 1.5 = integer 2
.1875 x 16 = 3   = 3/16th vulgar fraction
```

Key in the following **VUL/FRAC** * * formula:

VUL/FRAC:IF(S(VALUE) OR S(VULG?):RND(FP(V
ALUE)xBASE:0)-VULG?:VULG?÷BASE-FRAC)

(Ensure a space before/after OR above)
VALUE   BASE   VULG   FRAC

After obtaining the "first try" uneven number, press [FRAC] to check how near the resulting fraction is to the requirement. If necessary try again with a higher/lower base number. Below are two example:

VALUE	BASE	VULG	FRAC		
96.1875	64	?			
		= 12			

VALUE	BASE	VULG	FRAC		
	32	?			
		= 6			

VALUE	BASE	VULG	FRAC		
	16	?	?		
		= 3	= .187500	= 96 & 3/16ths	

VALUE	BASE	VULG	FRAC		
2.4578	16	?	?		
		= 7	= .437500	= 2 & 7/16ths	

VALUE	BASE	VULG	FRAC		
	64	?	?		
		= 29	= .453125	= 2 & 29/64ths	

VALUE	BASE	VULG	FRAC		
	128	?	?		
		= 59	= .460938	= 2 & 59/128ths	

VALUE	BASE	VULG	FRAC		
	2	?	?		
		= 1	= .500000	= 2½	

Take your choice!

Agents' commissions

Agents' commissions inevitably vary according to the work which they do. Active assistance, with the agent having considerable expenses, is probably worth a higher fee than a mere introduction at an "old-boy" luncheon. The following formula may be useful to finance directors:

$$\frac{\text{Category} \times 20}{2 \times ((\text{LOG Capital Value}) - 1)} = \text{commission percentage}$$

The [LOG]s used in the formula above must be [LOG]s(10) *not* logs natural, [LN]

The "categories" are the prerogative of the finance director and can be anything from 1 (the lowest) up to any value he wishes.

If the capital value of the contract was worth, say, £250,000 and the agent was category 2, the equation would be:

$$\frac{2 \times 20}{2 \times ((\text{LOG } 250,000) - 1)} = 4.55$$

In the case of a transaction of (say) £100,000 where the finance director decided that the agent was category 3, the interest rate would be 7.50% and the amount (cash) due is £7,500. Alternatively, another agent, working on a £125,000 project, which had been successfully launched at considerable cost to himself, might be considered to be category 6, and his percentage would thus be 14.645184 with cash due of some £18,306.48 If, by agreement this was curtailed to 14% the amount due would reduce to £17,500.

Key in the following **AGENTS** * * program:

```
AGENTS:IF(S(CAT#) OR S(COM%):CAT#x20÷((LO
G(VALUE)-1)x2)-COM%:(VALUExCOM%÷100)-CASH)
```

(Ensure a space before/after OR above)

CAT# VALUE COM% CASH

and taking the above examples:

CAT#	VALUE	COM%	CASH
3	100000	?	
		= 7.50	?
			=7,500

CAT#	VALUE	COM%	CASH
6	125000	?	
		= 14.65	?
			=18,306.48

If the finance director cut this percentage to a 14% commission the amount due becomes:

CAT#	VALUE	COM%	CASH
		14	?
			=17,500

The profitability index

This index, widely used in the States, is the present value of the anticipated cash flows discounted at the investor's required yield, all divided by the initial investment.

$$\frac{\text{Present Value Cash Flows}}{\text{Initial Investment}} = PI$$

If the PI is greater than 1 the investor's required yield has been exceeded, consequently in the program below an input of 1 to the [PI] label will provide the correct cash flow yield.

A short program **[PI]** can be keyed-in if desired:

```
[PI]:SGN(TERM)x((USPV(YLD%:TERM)xSGN(COST
)xINCM)+(SOLDx(SPFV(YLD%:-TERM))))÷COST=[
PI]
```

TERM	YLD%	COST	INCM	SOLD	[PI]

Taking an example from the HP-12C *Real Estate Applications Handbook*: assume that a purchase with an original cost of $10,000, and with an annual income of $1,580, was sold after 7 years for $7,500. If the investor requires a rate of return of 13% what is the profitability index?

TERM	YLD%	COST	INCM	SOLD	[PI]
7	13	10000	1580	7500	? = 1.017568

and what is the true yield of the investment and subsequent cash flows if the [PI] is 1?

TERM	YLD%	COST	INCM	SOLD	[PI]
	?				1

= 13.428782%

The factor [PI] was surrounded in the program and in the menu label by [ ] to avoid confusion with the HP [MATH] menu where PI represents "π", namely 3.141593.

The π factor.

A comment, which admittedly has absolutely nothing to do with rate interest, or anything else, for that matter, connected with Hewlett-Packard calculators!

In most modern scientific calculators a key to obtain π is usually provided, but not so on the cheaper conventional vest pocket credit card type calculator that many carry in their wallet or filofax.

To obtain the π value, somewhat more accurately than the old school factor of 22/3, divide the inverse of the first half into the second half of the first three doubled uneven numbers:

$$\frac{1}{113/355} = 3.14159292035$$

against the HP [PI] key in the [MATHS] mode = 3.14159265359

– a difference of only some 0.0000002

CHAPTER 2

Some Formulae and Actuarial Signs

Actuarial shorthand
The presentation of formulae, mathematical legends and languages naturally differs from country to country. Actuaries, however, have a form of shorthand which can be extremely useful in reducing the length of well-known formulae – saving space and often assisting clarity of thought. This shorthand will be used on many occasions in the following pages.

Compounding and discounting
£100 invested for 10 years at 10% at simple interest means that each year the lender receives 100 x .10 = £10

Readers will appreciate that if a lender does not wish to receive the interest every year but "leaves it with the borrower", what the lender is, in fact, doing is to re-lend to the borrower the interest engendered the previous year. The problem is to calculate the future value of the loan at the end of the term.

An interest rate referred to as percentage is (say) 10% but when set out in a formula is divided by 100, shown as a decimal and referred to as "i": for example 10% is shown as .10 = i.

If compounding occurs, then the number of "rests", or compounding periods, in any *one* year is referred to as the "p" factor.

Consequently 10% interest, compounded monthly, converted to a decimal fraction becomes 10/1200 = 0.008333 and in formulae this figure is referred to as "i/p".

The value "n" refers to the number of years in the term. Thus if an interest rate is compounded over a term of n years the method is to divide the percentage value by both 100 and the number of periodic (p) rests in any one year, add 1 and raise the result to the power of n.

If 10% is compounded *annually* over a term of 25 years the equation would be presented as:

$$(1 + i)^n \quad \text{or } (1 + i)\hat{~}n \text{ or sometimes } (1 + i)**n$$
$$1.10^{25} \quad \text{or} \quad 1.10\hat{~}25 \quad \text{or } 1.10**25$$

If the interest is compounded *monthly* the equation becomes:

$$(1 + i/p)^{np} \quad \text{or } (1 + i/p)\hat{~}np$$
$$(1 + 10/12)^{300} \quad \text{or } 1.0008333\hat{~}25\times12$$

Thus the value of £100 at the end of 25 years compounded at a rate of 10% nominal is:

$$100(1 + 10/1200)^{25\times12} = 1{,}205.69$$
$$£100(1 + i)\hat{~}n = 100(1 + .10)^{10} = £259.37$$

Employing the Business Calculators' [TVM] discipline the above example would present as:

[MAIN]	FIN	TVM	OTHER	1	P/YP	END	[EXIT]
N	I%YR	PV	PMT	FV	OTHER		
25x12	10/12	−100	0	?	FV = 1,205.69		

or alternatively press [OTHER] 12 press [P/YR]:

N	I%YR	PV	PMT	FV	OTHER
300	10	−100	0	?	FV = 1,205.69

The [PV] above is negative as a result of Hewlett-Packard's cash flow assumption that if a borrower makes payments to a lender he is "out of pocket" for that amount, and the payments will thus be shown as a negative in the [TVM] discipline. Conversely, a lender, treating payment(s) received as positive, may need to make an "out of pocket" payment at the end of the term, if so the [FV] must be negative.

It does not matter which perspective is used, but it is vital to be consistent; especially so far as deposits, withdrawals and balloon payments are concerned.

It is good practice to commence fresh program calculations with ▌ [CLEAR DATA] but as many calculations are usually continuous, with previous values remaining *in situ*, remember always to input zero into any register not required for that particular calculation.

Discounting is merely compounding in reverse. Your great aunt leaves you £5,000 in ten years' time and instead of waiting for your inheritance you want to "cash in" now. Providing you can get someone to give you the cash now you can spend the money – now.

As a "banker" will not receive the £5,000 until the end of 10 years, he will only give you what he considers that amount is worth *now*. If the current lending rate, the "going rate", is 10% then all you will get is just under £2,000 to spend *now*:

$$5,000/(1 + i)^n \quad = \quad PV$$
$$\text{or} \quad 5,000/(1 + i)\char94 n \quad = \quad PV$$
$$\text{or} \quad 5,000/1.10**10 \quad = \quad 1,927.72$$

An alternative method of calculating discounting, much favoured in formulae, is by the use of the negative power, with the value multiplied rather than divided, for example:

$$5,000 \times 1.10^{-10} = 1,927.72$$

▌ [MAIN]	FIN	TVM	OTHER	1	P/YP	END	[EXIT]
N	I%YR	PV	PMT	FV	OTHER		
10	10	?	0	5000	PV = −1,927.72		

The actuarial sign for this negative factor $(1 + i/p)\char94 {-n}$ is "v", in other words the *discount* sign. Consequently –v represents the compounding factor of $(1 + i)\char94 n$. As this can be confusing to those not dealing with such matters on a day-to-day basis, in the following pages the full $(1 + i/p)$ will always be used even when, in some cases, the rate concerned is annual with no periodic rests. For in this case p = 1.

Repayment loans

The formula for repayment, or mortgage type, loans is:

$$\text{Repayments} \times \frac{[1 - (1 + i/p)^{-np}]}{i/p} = \text{Loan}$$

$$\text{Loan} \div \frac{[1 - (1 + i/p)^{-np}]}{i/p} = \text{Pmts}$$

and the acturarial sign for the above factor is $a_{\overline{np}|}$

$$\frac{\text{loan}}{a_{\overline{np}|}} \text{ at } x\% = \text{pmts} \quad \text{or} \quad \text{pmts } a_{\overline{np}|} \text{ at } x\% = \text{loan}$$

As readers will be aware, repayment loans, of the mortgage type, require repayments to be made "in arrears", which is technically called "annuities *ordinary*", and is denoted on the HP Business Calculators by [END MODE].

If, therefore, we had a simple repayment loan of, say, £10,000.00 over a term of 25 years at a nominal rate of 11%, with monthly payments, the formula/equation would be:

$$\frac{10,000.00}{a_{\overline{300}|}} \text{ at } 11\% \text{ nominal (monthly)}$$
$$\text{or} \quad \text{at } (11/12)\%$$

£10,000 ÷ [(1 − 1.009167^−300)/.009167] =
£10,000 ÷ [(1 − 0.064734)   /.009167] =
£10,000 ÷   (.935266/.009167) =
£10,000 ÷ 102.029044 (loan ÷ factor) = £98.011308 pmts monthly

and the above, employing the [TVM] discipline, would be:

N	I%YR	PV	PMT	FV	
300	11÷12	−10000	?	0	PMT = 98.01 pmts in arrears

To find the factor 102.03, sometimes very necessary:

```
[INPUT] [-] 1 to PMT
   N      I%YR    PV      PMT      FV
  300    0.91667   ?      -1        0
                  = 102.029044
```

Alternatively:

a___ factor multiplied by the payments = 98.01 x 102.03 = 10,000 loan
 n |

When we come to consider leasing it will be seen that the repayments are in advance, one payment being made as soon as the contract commences. This is called "annuities *due*", and is executed on the HP calculators by employing [BEGIN MODE]. The above repayment formula stands as set out except that the payments are divided by $(1 + i/p)$.

The actuarial sign for annuities due has two dots above the letter "a" thus:

a___ (ord)   ä___ (due)
 np | p |

```
■ [MAIN]   FIN    TVM    OTHER  12  P/YR   BEG    [EXIT]
    N      I%YR    PV      PMT        FV
   300     11    -10000     ?          0     PMT = 97.12 pmts in advance
```

To construct a program covering the above actuarial formula, key in the following:

$$SGN(N) \times USPV(I\% \div P : N \times P) = LOAN \div (-PMTS)$$

```
       N      I%      P    LOAN    PMTS
      25      11     12   -10000     ?
                                 =  98.01 (END)
              [÷] [(] 11 [÷] 1200 [+] 1 [=] 97.12 (BEGIN)
```

The sGN(N) at the beginning of the program, as explained in the Introduction, has no mathematical significance and was included merely to locate [N] as the first box in the menu.

CHAPTER 3

Annuities Ordinary and Due

General

In the last chapter we saw how annuities ordinary [END] and due [BEGIN] (payments in arrears or in advance) were represented by the actuarial symbols below:

```
a____   or  ä____    respectively.
  np |        np |
```

We know that rounding to 2 decimal places for payments and other "cash" values may affect other values in an equation and can sometimes lead to decimal discrepancies.

```
          10,000
          98.01a_____   at (11/12)%
                 300 |
```

[MAIN]	FIN	TVM	OTHER	12	P/Y	END	[EXIT]
N	I%YR	PV	PMT	FV	OTHER	and adjust)	
300	11	−10000	?	0			

=98.01 ▌ [SHOW] 98.0113076917

N	I%YR	PV	PMT	OTHER
300	?	−10000	98.01	0

=10.999819 rounded

Does this mean that if the APR of 11% nominal is correctly stated as 11.5% the whole requirement will have to be re-calculated if the payments are rounded? Fortunately, no. It was this problem which led to the decision to *truncate* the effective rate to one place of decimals and call it the APR. Mind you, this does not absolve the statistician from re-calculating if a major change occurs in the structure of the loan, such as the addition of a front-end fee.

Balances annuities ordinary pmts [END]

A balance, or the "loan outstanding" (LOS), can be found for any loan by finding the [FV]. Taking the previous loan and employing the values already input in the [TVM] line of keys, find the LOS at the end of the 22nd year (264th period):

N	I%YR	PV	PMT	FV	OTHER
264	11	−10,000	98.01	?	
				= 2,995.19	

Pressing ▌ [SHOW] will produce the figure 2,995.18713326

The calculations are thus seen to be always at the full precision of the calculator.

In many cases the [FV], once found, will be re-employed in another calculation and in that case the full precision is correct; but if the balance is, metaphorically, to be "paid out in cash", then the correct procedure is to use the amortisation [AMRT] facility. For in this case the values, balances, interest and other available data are all "rounded" according to the decimal [FIX] since this discipline is a schedule and not a calculation. Therefore cash payouts should have a decimal setting of 2.

Assuming that the calculation above is retained in the calculator, find a quick balance by the [AMRT] discipline at the end of the 264th month. It is important to ensure that the decimal [FIX] is 2 when using [AMRT].

N	I%YR	PV	PMT	FV	press OTHER press	AMRT
#P	INT	PRIN	BAL	NEXT	TABLE	
264			?			
			= 2,995.43 Press ▌ [SHOW] = 2,995.43			

Balances annuities due pmts [BEGIN]

With payments in advance the balances are assumed to be those at the beginning of each period under review, ready to accept the interest for the following period. So if the [FV] key in the [TVM] discipline is employed to find the balances divide the result by (1 + i/p). Amortisation, the [AMRT] discipline, finds the periodic balances by schedule methods.

With £1,000 at 11% with £100 advance payments:

```
1000.00              -100      = 900      (balance at   commencement)
( 900.00 x 1.11) -100          = 899      (  "      beginning year 2)
( 899.00 x 1.11) -100          = 897.89 (  "          "       " 3)
```

N	I%YR	PV	PMT	FV	OTHER	1 P/YR	BEG	[EXIT]
ignore	11	-1000	100	0				

AMRT	#P	INT	PRIN	BAL	NEXT	TABLE
3				?		

= 897.89

and this is confirmed by the [CFLO] discipline:

```
[MAIN]   FIN   CFLO   [CLEAR DATA] = CLEAR THE LIST?   YES
FLOW(0)=?
1000 [-] 100 [=] [+/-] [INPUT]
FLOW(1)? 100 [INPUT]
#TIMES(1)= 2 [INPUT]
[EXIT] CALC  11  I%   NFV =-897.89 [EXIT] [EXIT]
```

Compare the [FIN] [TVM] discipline. Ensure 1 [P/YR] and [BEG].

N	I%YR	PV	PMT	FV
3	11	-1000	100	?

= 996.66 [÷] 1.11 = 897.89

How to find the interest? The capital balance for any period less the balance for the next period must equal the capital repaid for the intervening period, and so if that amount is deducted from the payments made during that period the result must be the total interest paid.

N	I%YR	PV	PMT	FV
2	11	-1000	100	?

= 997.89 [÷] 1.11 [=] 899.00

N	I%YR	PV	PMT	FV
3				?

= 996.66 [÷] 1.11 [=] 897.89

899.00 [-] 897.89 [-] 100 [=] -98.89

OTHER   AMRT 1 #P   NEXT   NEXT   INT = interest = 98.89

24   **Chapter 3**

Odd days
Inevitably the structure of real life loans often differs from book theory! Lending institutions, with computer accounting, usually prefer all their repayments to be made on a particular date, such as mid- or end-month. In that case there are often some "odd days" which have to be taken into account.

If the payments are monthly and the first payment is due on, say, July 1 and the advance is made 8 days before that date, there will be 8 odd days' interest to be accounted for. In effect, what is happening is that, irrespective of the main loan, the borrower is taking out a secondary loan just for the odd days – at the original rates.

For example, if the loan was for £1,000 at a rate of 10% nominal, with monthly payments required, the 8 days' interest due would be 1,000 x (10/1200 x 8 x 12/365) = £2.19, working on the actual calendar; or x 8/30 employing the 30/360 calendar, making £2.22 interest. In this event the loan is no longer £1,000 but becomes £1,000 plus the interest above and, given the rate, the new payments can be determined. Conversely, given these payments the the rate can be found by a program.

In the States the interest is more often found from the quoted "flat rate" and, in that case, the interest engendered is divided by the number of payments due and added to the conventional non-odd-day payments.

In the UK the interest is often found by compound means rather than, as above, by simple interest methods:

$$1,000 \times (1+10/1200)^{(8\times12/365)} = £1,002.185083$$

An example, given some years ago, for the HP-67/97 series of calculators was as follows: a 36 month car loan for $3,500 with a 6% "add-on rate" (in the UK, the simple interest rate!) is initiated so that there are 18 odd days. Calculate the monthly repayments required to amortise this loan, the total finance charge, and the "annual percentage rate" (in the UK the nominal rate%).

The payments are:

$$(3,500 + (3,500 \times 6/100 \times 3))/36 = \$114.72 \text{ pmts}$$

and for the odd days:

$$3,500 \times 6/100 \times 18/360 \qquad = \quad 10.50$$
$$\text{and} \quad 10.50/36 + 114.72 \qquad = \$115.01 \text{ pmts}$$

The program below provides the nominal rate as 10.880593%, assuming simple interest calculations and annuities ordinary, namely [END] mode; the total finance charge being:

$$(115.01 \times 36) - 3,500 = \$640.36$$

Given the UK method, employing the actual calendar and at compound interest for the odd days, the rate is fractionally different from the above and is found as 10.886204%: the loan plus interest being:

$$£3,500 \times 1.009072^{\wedge}18 \times 12/365 = £3,518.76$$

The HP-19B *Manual*, page 246, outlines a program based on the financial calendar (30/360) and simple interest calculations, the [BEGIN] modes being incorporated in the program structure. But this program is not transportable to the 17B, consequently an odd days program is provided below which offers the facilities of choice, namely the various options of [BEGIN] and [END], compound or simple interest, and the actual or 30/360 calendars.

Key in the following **ODD/DAYS** program:

```
ODD/DAYS:(0xNxI%xPVxPMT)+IF(FP(N)=0:-PV-F
Vx(SPFV(I%:-N))):-PV-FVxSPFV(I%:-INT(N))+I
F(C=0:(-PVxI%÷100xFP(N)):-PVx(SPPV(I%:FP(
-N))-1)))÷IF(INT(N)=0:USPV(I%:N):USPV(I%:
INT(N)))=IF(INT(N)=0:0:PMTxIF(BEG=0:1:(1+
I%÷100)))
```

N	I%	PV	PMT	FV	MORE
C	BEG				MORE

The program provides for odd-days facilities when the [N] value contains a decimal fraction; the whole format being precisely similar to that of the HP-12C Financial Calculator – save that the input is by conventional means (not the *Reverse Polish Notation*). This resemblance may possibly appeal to those users updating from the 12C to the 17B.

The program defaults to [END] (annuities ordinary) and simple interest modes when ▌ [CLEAR DATA] is employed, since zero is then lodged in the registers [BEG] and [C] (for compound interest).

To convert to [BEGIN] mode, input 1 to [BEG] and 1 to [C] for compound interest calculations. (This discipline is designed to equate with the HP-12C method of keying-in [g] [BEG] to convert to [BEGIN] mode and the "toggle" key routine of [STO] [EEX] = c both appearing as status indicators on display.)

The general input follows the method employed by the HP in-built [TVM] program, but assumes an annual perspective throughout; consequently for monthly terms the annual [N] factor must be multiplied by 12 and the nominal [I%] factor divided by 12 (resembling the HP-12C method).

The input for loans and instalments conforms to the HP convention whereby the "in" payments (receipts) are positive and payments "out" negative (see page 53, HP-17B *Manual*; page 78, HP-19B *Manual*).

Taking the example on page 24, the [N] factor is:

$$18 \ [\text{x}] \ 12 \ [\div] \ 360 \ [+] \ 36 \ [=] \ 36.60$$

N	I%	PV	PMT	FV	MORE
36.60	?	−3500	115.01	0	
C	BEG				
0	0			I% =	0.906716
				[x] 12 [=]	10.880593 Nominal

Assume a loan of $6,000 over a period of 36 months at a true nominal rate of 13.50%. The loan will have a month and five odd days before the first payment is due. This example is taken from the 17B *Manual* (page 160).

The [N] factor is:

5 [×] 12 [÷] 360 [+] 36 [=] 36.16667 and 13.5 [÷] 12 [=] 1.125

Press [I%]:

N	I%	PV	PMT	FV	MORE
36.16667	1.125	−6000	?	0	
C	BEG		= 203.99		
0	0				

In relation to the program for the HP-19B, mentioned above, the *Manual's* explanation possibly lacks HP's usual clarity.

The HP-12C calculator (and indeed the above program) had a special [N] key facility for finding data related to odd day calculations. The *Owner's Handbook* explained the whole procedure and method of calculating odd day payments both concisely and clearly: the options for [BEGIN/END] and compound and simple interest modes being part of the main calculator format. "The odd period, therefore, cannot be greater than one regular period", they say – meaning that if a month is 30 days the odd days must be less than 30 days, a view with which it is difficult to quarrel.

But on page 246 of the 19B *Manual*, which previously states that a month is taken as 30 days, the following example is outlined: "A 36-month loan for $4,500 has an annual interest rate of 15%. If the first payment is made in 46 days, what is the monthly payment?"

In the program provided, 46 days is keyed into the [DAYS] input and the answer given is $157.03. At the same time a note states "If the odd period is less than 30 days [BEGIN] mode is assumed. If the period is between 30 and 59 days, inclusive, [END] mode is assumed."

What the authors mean, presumably, is that there are 30 days plus 16 odd days to the first payment, consequently they assume that payments are in arrears, whereas in the next example where there are 8 days to first payment, they assume that payments must be in advance. They have therefore written their program to take account of these assumptions.

Are there not times, perhaps, when one can do almost too much to help the user? I for one, knowing, as one always would, if the loan had an advance payment, would prefer to input the correct number of odd days and then, when and if necessary, adjust my program to [BEGIN] or [END] as required.

Furthermore the HP program outlined in both *Manuals* is designed only to cover monthly payments, the 30/360 calendar and simple interest discounting, whereas in Europe the "actual" 365 calendar, compounding discounting and, sometimes, payments other than monthly are required.

Consequently, as an alternative to the HP program I can but suggest that users of the 19B consider employing the ODD/DAYS program, supplied above, for this covers the whole range of US and European requirements.

(See also Appendix VI)

Taking the above 19B example where the [N] factor is:

16 [x] 12 [÷] 360 [+] 36 [=]   36.53333 press   N

and   15 [÷] 12 [=]   1.25   press   I%

N	I%	PV	PMT	FV	MORE
36.5333	1.25	−4500	?	0	
C	BEG		= 157.033938		
0	0				

A second example, with a balloon payment, was also provided, namely: "A $10,000 loan has 24 monthly payments of $400, plus a balloon payment of $3,000 at the end of the 24th month. If the payments begin in 8 days what annual interest is being charged?"   From the way the example is drafted one can but assume the payments are intended to be in advance and therefore in [BEGIN] mode. The given answer is 19.67%.

The [N] factor is:

8 [x] 12 [÷] 360 [+] 24 [=]   24.266667

N	I%	PV	PMT	FV	MORE
24.2667	?	−10000	400	3000	

C	BEG			I% =	1.639471
0	1			[x] 12 [=] 19.673647 Nominal	

Taking the same example, but using European methods, the [N] factor now is:

8 [x] 12 [÷] 365 [+] 24 [=]   24.263014

N	I%	PV	PMT	FV	MORE
24.2630	?	−10000	400	3000	

C	BEG			I% =	1.640105
1	1			[x] 12 [=] 19.681260 Nominal	

Calculations on the TVM program

Loans, in practice, come in all shapes and sizes and often their structures are almost unrecognisable when compared to the conventional types of loans which are used in most books of instruction.   The HP *Manuals*, employing the [FIN] [TVM] discipline, outline the normal, conventional loans, savings and leasings.

But this program has many other applications and can calculate loans which at first sight appear so complex as to require a special computer program to resolve them. Just two examples are given below.

A bridging loan of £30,000 for a nominal six months at 2% monthly interest. The interest is deducted from the capital amount at the time of the drawdown, a processing fee of £150 and a single endowment insurance premium of £750 is also deducted at drawdown. Find the UK APR.

If you think about it, as the interest has been paid front end, there are no payments, but the capital has to be repaid at the end of the 6 months. Is this not therefore a simple and uncomplicated compound interest sum?

The loan the borrower actually receives is £30,000 – (30,000 x .02 x 6) = £26,400, and less £150 and less £750, which equals £25,500

FIN	TVM				
N	I%YR	PV	PMT	FV	OTHER
6	?	−25500	0	30000	(12 P/YR BEG MODE on display)
	= 32.947994%				

and with 32.947994 on display, to find the effective rate:

[÷] 1200 [+] 1 [y^x] 12 [−] 1 [x] 100 = 38.41% effective
　　　　　　　　　　　　　　　　　　= 38.4% APR

Another problem, from Australia this time. The "amount financed" is Aust\$13,991.15 and the term is 48 months. The true (nominal) rate of interest is 26.82%　The client pays A\$100 monthly for the first 6 months, A\$467.33 monthly for the next 36 months, how much does he need to pay monthly for the last 6 months?

Again using the invaluable "top line of keys":

N	I%YR	PV	PMT	FV	OTHER	12	P/YR	END
6	26.82	−13991.15	100	?	FV = 15,340.83 [+/−]			
36		−15340.83	467.33	?	FV = 8,568.71 [+/−]			
6		− 8568.71	?	0	PMT = 1,541.89			

Wrap around loans

The wrap around is, in effect, a secondary loan; a loan re-financed so that the borrower, receiving the difference between the present value of his existing mortgage and the capital value of the new loan, has more cash to spend, on (say) home improvements. The mortgagor covering the new loan need not be the same one as for the original loan. If a new mortgagor is involved, he now owns the whole loan and is responsible for paying the first lender the original repayments, taking from the borrower sufficient instalments to cover both the original repayments and the new capital injected into the existing loan.　Should the borrower fail the second lender is still responsible for the original installments.

The wrap around loan calculations are fully covered in the HP *Real Estate, Banking and Leasing* pamphlet relating to the HP-17B, 19B and 27S calculators. The HP program necessitates moving to and from the [TVM] program; this irritation can be avoided if the method below is employed.

The program below is the same as the HP program, save that the menu has been re-arranged, the nomenclature reselected and the discipline altered. Perhaps it may prove useful.

Key in the following **WRAP** program:

WRAP:(P-P)+LOAN-(PMTSxSGN(#PER)-(BAL-BAL)
)xSGN(P)x(USPV(YLD÷P:#PER))-BALx(SPPV(YLD
÷P:#PER))=WRAP-WPMTx(USPV(YLD÷P:WPER))-WB
ALx(SPPV(YLD÷P:WPER))

P	LOAN	PMTS	#PER	BAL	MORE
YLD	WRAP	WPMT	WPER	WBAL	MORE

The [YLD] factor is shared between the original loan and the secondary wrap around loan (with the prefix of "W").

As an example take a loan with an existing balance of $125,010, with 200 payments of $1,051.61 to run to maturity. The secondary loan required is for $200,000, at 9.5% with 240 monthly payments of $1,681.71,and a balloon payment at the end of the term of $129,963.35 If a secondary lender accepts these terms what would be the rate of return (yield)?

Assuming that the secondary 240 payments of $1,681.71 were *not* known: to find these payments, which are in the second portion of the program, the relative values in the primary portion of the program/menu must be ignored, so store the balance and payments for the primary values, the *existing* loan, for later use: 125,010 [STO 1] and 1051.61 [STO 2].

P	LOAN	PMTS	#PER	BAL	MORE
12	0	0	0	0	
YLD	WRAP	WPMT	WPER	WBAL	MORE
9.5	200000	?	240	129963.35	

= 1,681.709978 (round 2 places and reinput)

To find the rate of return re-constitute the program:

P	LOAN	PMTS	#PER	BAL	MORE
12	[RCL1]	[RCL2]	200	0	

YLD	WRAP	WPMT	WPER	WBAL	MORE
?	200000	1,681.71	240	129963.35	

= 11.839092 = 11.84% rate of return

(see HP's *Estate,Banking and Leasing Solutions Book*, page 56)

If it was decided that the rate of return had to be precisely 12% what new instalments would the borrower need to pay monthly and what would be the interest rate?

P	LOAN	PMTS	#PER	BAL	MORE
12	125010	1051.61	200	0	

YLD	WRAP	WPMT	WPER	WBAL	MORE
12	200000	?	240	129963.35	

= 1,693.97

To find the rate of return, which affects only the secondary part of the program, clear registers [LOAN] and [PMTS].

P	LOAN	PMTS	#PER	BAL	MORE
12	0	0	0	0	

YLD	WRAP	WPMT	WPER	WBAL	MORE
?	200000	1,693.97	240	129963.35	

= 9.58% rate of return

(see HP's *Estate,Banking and Leasing Solutions Book*, page 57)

A mortgage loan on an income property has a current balance of $200,132.06. When the loan originated 8 years ago, it had a 20 year term with level monthly payments and an interest rate of 6.75%. A lender has agreed to wrap a $300,000 second mortgage at 10% with equal payments over 12 years. What is the yield to the lender on the net cash advanced?

It will be appreciated that the question makes no mention of the monthly payments required for either the original or the new loan; so before attempting to calculate anything these payments must be found.

The remaining term for the original loan is 20 – 8 years and multiplied by 12 = 144 months. Now key in 200,132.06 and [STO 0] and input to [LOAN]:

P	LOAN	PMTS	#PER	BAL	MORE
12	200132.06	?	144	0	
		= 2,031.55	[STO 1]		

YLD	WRAP	WPMT	WPER	WBAL	MORE
6.75	0	0	0	0	

and for the new loan:

P	LOAN	PMTS	#PER	BAL	MORE
12	0	0	144	0	

YLD	WRAP	WPMT	WPER	BAL	MORE
10	300000	?	144	0	
		= 3,585.23			

and now putting together both loans:

P	LOAN	PMTS	#PER	BAL	MORE
12	[RCL0]	[RCL1]	144	0	

YLD	WRAP	WPMT	WPER	WBAL	MORE
?	300000	3,585.23			
= 15.85% nominal yield to the lender					

(see HP's *Estate,Banking and Leasing Solutions Book*, page 58)

Cash flows

Discounted cash flow (DCF) calculations are extremely valuable as a check on any abnormal loan structure, and the [CFLO] discipline is fully explained in the *Manuals*. Taking the first wrap around example which had two terms, namely 200 and 240 months, the cash flows would be as follows:

The investment would be £125,010 – 200,000 (input as a negative). The payments would be £1,681.71 – 1051.61 for 200 months, and £1,681.71 for 39 months (found from (240 – 200) – 1) then £1,681.71 + 129,963.35 (the balloon) for 1 month. This will provide an IRR of 11.84% (see the first example).

The golden handshake

Often much of the controversy regarding the amounts due to be paid for the loss of office (be it for the low paid worker or for top management) stems from a failure to understand the mathematics and the concept behind such payouts.

If a company executive, at whatever level, having a contract to be retained by the company for certain number of years, is suddenly dismissed from that company through no fault of his or her own, the company, in all fairness, is liable to pay some compensation.

It is the amount of compensation due for the loss of office which is often open to question.

The generally accepted concept is that the amount of compensation paid should *if invested* represent, and be equivalent to, the amount of the pay and emoluments which the executive would have received annually if he or she had not been dismissed.

The legal arguments usually revolve round two issues: namely the amount of extra emoluments, apart from the basic pay, which the executive enjoyed during his time with the company *and* the rate of return (the percentage) on the (hypothetical) investment. Paradoxically, the higher the rate the lower the compensation, consequently the company will usually argue for the rate to be "near the banks' lending rate", the opposing view probably being "about 5%". Why is this?

Assume that a middle level executive is receiving, say, £50,000 per year, which includes all extras such as attractive mortgage rates, cars, childrens' schooling, BUPA, etc, and that he has a service agreement contract which ties him to the company for 5 years. Through no fault of his own, he is suddenly dismissed after 2 years.

The compensation must therefore be such that he can invest the cash, whatever it is, immediately on receipt, in order to receive £50,000 for the next three years.

The calculation is quite simply a "repayment loan" over a term, the pay and emoluments being treated as the "payments" and the compensation amount as the "loan amount". As the investment must necessarily be immediate as soon as the compensation is received the calculation must be payments in advance, annuities *due*, namely [BEGIN].

■ [MAIN]	SOLVE	FIN	TVM			
N	I%YR	PV	PMT	FV	OTHER	(ensure 1 P/YR and BEGIN)
3	10	?	−50000	0		
		=£136,777				

If the investment rate was 5%:

N	I%YR	PV	PMT	FV	OTHER
3	5	?	−50000	0	
		=£142,971			

The capital amount required, and thus the compensation, must obviously be greater if the return on the investment obtainable returns only 5%, roughly the yield on ordinary shares, rather than returning 10%.

Mathematics versus practice
Suppose that in the above example the term to run was not three years but two and a half years. In this case the [N] value would be 2.5 and consequently *because of the fraction* the user would immediately consider employing the odd days calculation outlined earlier.

But it will be found that in practice this is not realistic, so the [TVM] program must be employed. HP correctly comments (page 53, HP-17B: page 77, HP-19B *Manuals*) that the results of a calculation employing the [TVM] program with an [N] value having a decimal fraction must be interpreted carefully in that, "while mathematically correct the result has no simple interpretation".

For the result of using such a calculation is to divide the payment periods into even periods related to the [N] value. Using the [TVM] program for a problem with odd days calculation would normally be absurd – but with exactly half a period it is legitimate.

N	I%YR	PV	PMT	FV	OTHER
3	10	?	−50000	0	
		=£136,777			
2.5		=£116,608			
	2	=£ 95,455			
	5	=£120,571			

Whereas using the ODD/DAYS program:

	[MAIN]	SOLVE	↓↑	ODD/DAYS	CALC			

N	I%	PV	PMT	FV	MORE	C	BEG
3	10	?	−50000	0		1	1
		=£136,777					
2.5		=£ 91,012					
2		=£ 95,455					

Obviously employing the odd-days method here is ridiculous, since the capital value for 2½ years is *less* than that for 2 years!

CHAPTER 4

Less Conventional Loan Methods

Rule 78 or "sum of the digits" calculation
The correct name for this type of calculation is "sum of the digits" (or, nowadays, more politely the sum of the *years'* digits – SOYD), for "Rule 78" only really applies to *one* year, namely 12 months. Since $1+2+3+4+5+6+4+5+6+8+9+10+11+12$ = 78 (or 12 x 13/2 = 78). A two year loan, as will be seen from the loan example below, is not literally Rule 78 but 24 x 25/2 = 300 (SOYD)

This method of calculating repayment loans was used almost exclusively before the advent of computers, for it is based on simple interest calculations and can find the value of the monthly payments and balances without the necessity of finding the true rate of interest.

But while it is still used extensively in the USA, the UK Credit Consumer Act requires the disclosure of the APR(UK), and as this entails the calculation of the loan by actuarial means, there seems less and less point in employing the so–called simpler methods of calculation. Except for one important requirement; namely the Consumer Credit Act regulations concerning "penalties" for early redemption of a loan when it becomes necessary to use the Rule 78 method. For such calculations and a PENALTY/RULE78 program, see the Appendix, page 186.

Assume a loan of £3,000, over a term of 24 months, at a simple interest quoted rate of 6%. The charge is £3,000 x 6(%) x 2(yrs) ÷ 100 = £360.00, consequently the monthly repayments must be (3000 + 360) ÷ 24 (months) = £140.

From an examination of the table below it will be seen that interest paid is also reduced by a factor of charge/SOYD, namely 360/300 = 1.20

Sum of the Digits Schedule

Loan £3000.00   Term 24 Months   Flat rate 6%
True rate 11.126664%

Months	Interest paid	Capital repaid	Capital balances	Actuarial Equivalent
1	28.80	111.20	3000.00	2,887.82
2	27.60	112.40	2888.80	2,774.59
3	26.40	113.60	2662.80	2,660.32
4	25.20	114.80	2548.00	2,544.99
5	24.00	116.00	2432.00	2,428.58
6	22.80	117.20	2314.80	2,311.10
7	21.60	118.40	2196.40	2,192.53
8	20.40	119.60	2076.80	2,072.86
9	19.20	120.80	1956.00	1,952.08
10	18.00	122.00	1834.00	1,830.18
11	16.80	123.20	1710.80	1,707.15
12	15.60	126.40	1586.40	1,582.98
13	14.40	125.60	1460.80	1,457.66
14	13.20	126.80	1334.00	1,331.17
15	12.00	128.00	1206.00	1,203.52
16	10.80	129.20	1076.80	1,074.68
17	9.60	130.40	946.40	944.64
18	8.40	131.60	814.80	813.40
19	7.20	132.80	682.00	680.94
20	6.00	134.00	548.00	547.26
21	4.80	135.20	412.80	412.33
22	3.60	136.40	276.40	276.15
23	2.40	137.60	138.80	138.71
24	1.20	138.80	0.00	0.00
	360.00	3000.00		

The rebate and balances

From the table above it will be seen that the balance at the
end of the 5th month is £2,432.00, found by the formula below.
The rebate, the unearned interest, indicates the amount of
interest *not* paid to date. To find the rebate at the end of the
14th month add, from the table, the interest due from month
15 through to 24 = £66. The balance at the end of the 5th
month is £2,432.00

$$T \times \frac{I(T + 1)}{N(N + 1)} = \text{rebate}_n$$

$$(24 \times 14) \times \frac{360(24-14+1)}{24 \times 25} = £66.00 \quad \text{rebate}_{14}$$
$$(66.83)$$

$$PT - (\, I \times \frac{T(T+1)}{N(N+1)}\,) = \text{balance}_n$$

$$140(24-5) - 360(\, \frac{19 \times 20}{24 \times 25}\,) = £2,432.00 \; \text{balance}_5$$
$$(2,428.58)$$

The figures in brackets above represent the actuarial equivalent.

Key in the following programs **RULE78 * *** and
RULE78/INT:

```
RULE78:IF(S(RBATE) OR S(CHRG):RND(((NxSGN
(CHRG)-MTH?)x(2x(N-MTH?+1)÷(Nx(N+1))xCHRG
)÷2):2)-RBATE:RND(((N-MTH?)xPMTS-RBATE):2
)-BAL)
```

(Ensure a space before/after OR above)
N   CHRG   MTH?   RBATE   PMTS   BAL

```
RULE78/INT:RND(INV(Nx(N+1)÷2÷CHRG)x(N—MTH
?+1):2)=INT
```

N   CHRG   MTH?   INT

Taking the two examples above:

[MAIN] ↑↓ RULE 78 CALC (values are retained unless altered)

N	CHRG	MTH?	RBATE	PMTS	BAL
24	360	14	?		?
			=66.00	140	=1,334.00

N	CHRG	MTH?	RBATE	PMTS	BAL
		5	?		?
			=228.00		=2,432.00

If changing the MTH? the User MUST repress RBATE before pressing BAL

To find the interest for the 5th month:

```
charge ÷  sum of digits   = interest factor.
 360    ÷ ((24 x 25) ÷ 2) = 1.2
(namely each interest value differs by this amount)
(factor x (N  -  month? + 1) =        interest
( 1.2   x (24 -    5   + 1) = 24.00 interest
                                           m
                                           5
```

```
   [EXIT]   ↓↑    RULE78/INT   CALC
    N      CHRG    MTH?    INT
    24      360     5       ?
                         = 24.00
```

Constant payments to principal

This method of repaying both interest and capital for a repayment loan is structured by the principal being repaid in equal instalments, the outstanding interest being paid at the same time, consequently the periodic payments will be *uneven.*

With a loan of £1,000 over 10 years at 10% nominal the capital is repaid in even slices, namely 1,000/10 = £100, the interest being due on each periodic balance.

The schedule below shows how the interest is added at each period to the basic periodic capital repayment, with the consequent reduction of the amount interest payable with each instalment.

Year	Int due	Pmt to prin	Total per pmt	Balance
1	100	100	200	900
2	90	100	190	800
3	80	100	180	700
4	70	100	170	600
5	60	100	160	500
6	50	100	150	400
7	40	100	140	300
8	30	100	130	200
9	20	100	120	100
10	10	100	110	0
	550	1000	1550	

Key in the following **CPP** * * program:

```
CPP:IF(S(CPP) OR S(PMT):RND((SGN(LOAN)x(C
PP+I%÷100x(LOAN-(#PER-1)xCPP))):2)-PMT:RN
D((LOAN-#PERxCPP):2)-BAL)
```

(Ensure a space before/after OR above)

| LOAN | CPP | I% | #PER | PMT | BAL |

Find the 5th payment and the balance at the end of the 7th year from the above example:

LOAN	CPP	I%	#PER	PMT	BAL
1000	100	10	5	?	
				=160	
			7		?
					=300.00

Home loans - low start mortgage repayments

High interest lending rates, with consequent high periodic repayments, naturally cause considerable concern to home owners, especially the first time borrower, and many institutions have became adept at creating a variety of alternative methods to ease the burden. Below are examples of some of them.

The guiding concept is to have lower repayments at the start of the home loan on the assumption that, as the owner's pay and prospects increase over the years, he will become better able to afford the higher payments in the later years of the loan period.

Annual percentage uplifts

One of the most obvious ways of organising a low start loan with gradually rising payments is by having an annual percentage lift each year.

Payments are usually monthly, but the percentage increment is always annual: in other words the payments remain constant for 12 months before rising.

There are many useful variations on this type of calculation. Usually the percentage increment does not obtain throughout the full term of the loan, although it can of course do so if required. The conventional low start loan has rising levels of payments over (say) the first five years and from then on the payments remain at that level, or (more usually) one level higher.

The programs

The first program, LOAN/INCR, is based on the present value of a loan [PV] and determines the value of the payments if there is, or is not, an annual percentage increment. The [FV] can also be found in the second part of the program. The second program, LOAN/INCR/LIFT enables the user to determine the subsequent payments.

Key in the following two programs **LOAN/INCR * *** and **LOAN/INCR/LIFT**

```
LOAN/INCR:IF(S(PV)   OR   S(PMTS):RND(PV÷(U
SPV(RATE%÷P:P)xUSFV((((INCR÷100+1)÷SPFV(R
ATE%÷P:P))-1)xSGN(ΣYRS)x100:#YR?)+((USP
V(RATE%÷P:ΣYRSxP-#YR?xP)x(1+INCR÷100)^#
YR?)÷SPFV(RATE%÷P:Px#YR?)))):FIX)-PMTS:PVx
SPFV(RATE%÷P:PxΣYRS)-FV)
```

(Ensure a space before/after OR above)

PV	RATE%	P	INCR	ΣYRS	MORE
#YR?	FIX	PMTS	FV		MORE

```
LOAN/INCR/LIFT:SGN(#YR?)xRND((PMTSx(1+INC
R÷100)^(IF(#?>#YR?:INV(0):(#?-1)))):FIX)-
NEXT
```

#YR?	PMTS	INCR	#?	FIX	NEXT

INCR as the increment percentage lift each year
ΣYRS as the total number of years in the loan term
#YR? as the number of the year the lift is required cease
#? as the required year to find the NEXT pmt.

These two programs are, intentionally, similar in format and input requirements to those outlined in the next chapter, namely SAVINGS/INCR and SAVINGS/INCR/LIFT.

The LOAN/INCR values are shared by both programs so values need not be re-input after switching programs.

Two examples below are taken from the HP *Real Estate, Banking, and Leasing Solutions* pamphlet (for the HP-17B,19B, and 27S calculators – page 56).

Assume a loan of £50,000 over a term of 10 years. The rate of interest is 12½% and the annual increments are at 5%. Find the first payment if the payments are annual and rise each year for the full term of 10 years.

[MAIN]	SOLVE	↓↑	LOAN/INCR		CALC
PV	RATE%	P	INCR	ΣYRS	MORE
50000	12.50	1	5	10	
#YR?	FIX	PMTS	FV		
10	2	?			

= 7,524.26 annual

PV	RATE%	P	INCR	ΣYRS	MORE
50000	12.50	12	5	10	
#YR?	FIX	PMTS	FV		
10	2	?			

= 611.31   monthly

Next assume that the increment is still required for each of the ten years and find the payments for the 2nd and last period.

[EXIT]	↓↑	LOAN/INCR/LIFT			CALC
#YR?	PMTS	INCR	#?	FIX	NEXT
			2	2	?	= 641.88 (2nd pmt)
			10		?	= 948.34 (last pmt)

Now, taking the same loan and the same interest rate as before, assume that the term is 30 years and only the first 5 payments are required to increase.

[EXIT]	↓↑	LOAN/INCR	CALC		
PV	RATE%	P	INCR	ΣYRS	MORE
50000	12.50	12	5	30	
#YR?	FIX	PMTS	FV		
5	2	?			
		= 448.88			

What are the 3rd, 5th and final payments, if the 6th increment represents the on-going payments?

[EXIT]	↓↑	LOAN/INCR/LIFT	CALC		
#YR?	PMTS	INCR	#?	FIX	NEXT
			3	2	? = 494.89 (3rd pmt)
			5		? = 545.62 (5th pmt)
			6		? = SOLUTION NOT FOUND

(for the requirement was for a FIVE year left only)

6	(raising 1 year)	5	6		? = 545.616446
		6	2		? = 572.90 (6th pmt onward)
		7			? = SOLUTION NOT FOUND
		8			? = " " "

Out of interest, before losing the data input, assume a nil percentage increment, and input zero into [INCR]. It will be found that the first payment, and consequently every subsequent period payment, is £533.63. If the same data is input to the HP [TVM] discipline it will be found that the payments are, not unnaturally, the same!

The above are annuities ordinary [END], payments in arrears; if due [BEGIN], payments in advance, are required   divide by either $(1 + i)$ for annual, or $(1 + i/p)$ for monthly, payments.

HP examples

Two examples from the HP *Real Estate, Banking and Leasing Solutions* pamphlet (page 92) mentioned above. A 20 year annuity with a discount rate of 11.50%, paying $110 per month for the first year; the increment is 5.50% each year. What is the present value of the series of payments?

[EXIT]	↓↑	LOAN/INCR		CALC	
PV	RATE%	P	INCR	ΣYRS	MORE
?	11.5	12	5.5	20	
= 14,793.46					
#YR?	FIX	PMTS	FV		
20	11	110			

Note [FIX] 11. Always check the [FIX] label, especially after transferring from another program. When payments are *not* the requirement the [FIX] register should always hold 11, otherwise the peripheral findings may be slightly inaccurate.

Starting at the end of the year, you plan to make annual saving deposits into your account which is earning 13%, compounded annually. You plan to increase the amount of your deposit by 8% each year. If your first deposit is $1,200, how much will you accumulate over the next ten years?

PV	RATE%	P	INCR	ΣYRS	MORE
?	13	1	8	10	
= 8,736.14					
#YR?	FIX	PMTS	FV		
10	11	1200	0 (must be 0 to find the PV)		
then:			?		
			= 29,655.42 (fund accumulation)		

A further Hewlett-Packard example, for the HP-12C calculator: "You are appraising a piece of income property that is providing increasing rents. Assuming a 7% rate of increase over the next 5 years, what is the present value of the income stream? Your discount rate is 12%, rent for the first year is expected to be $8,500, and payments occur at the end of the year."

PV	RATE%	P	INCR	ΣYRS	MORE
?	12	1	7	5	

= 34,706.26

#YR?	FIX	PMTS	FV
5	11	8500	0

What is the rent in the last year?

[EXIT]	↓↑	LOAN/INCR/LIFT	CALC		
#YR?	PMTS	INCR	#?	FIX	NEXT
			5	2	?

= 11,141.77

6   = 11,141.766085

Two tier loans

Another method is to have a high and low rate.   Assume a £1,000 loan at a nominal 11% over 25 years (300 months).   If the first 3 years' payments were £7.00 per month (36 months) what are the remaining 22 years' (264 months) payments?

▌ [MAIN] FIN TVM OTHER 12 P/YR END [EXIT]

N	I%YR	PV	PMT	FV
36	11	−1000	7	?

= 1,091.92 [+/−]

N	I%YR	PV	PMT	FV
300−36	11	−1091.92	?	0 (don't forget the zero !)

=10.998042

round press PMT
11

To find the cross–over break–even month:

1000 press FV press N = 67.44 (68th month)

To find the loan outstanding at the end of the 120th month:

120 N 11 PMT FV = 876.92 LOS

Multi-tier payments

Assume a £7,000 loan over 25 years at 11% nominal. Assume, too, that the monthly payments rise £5 each 12 months and that the payments found by formula are those for the 6th year onward. What is the schedule of payments?

The payments for the years after the first five years are found from the following formula:

$$\frac{PV + [(a\underset{60\ |}{} + a\underset{48\ |}{} + a\underset{3\ |}{} + a\underset{2\ |}{} + a\underset{1\ |}{}) \times CL]}{a\underset{300\ |}{}} = \text{Last pmts}$$

where $1a\underset{n\ |}{}$ represents the annuities ordinary formula of:

$$1 \times [1 - (1 + i/p)^{-np}]/(i/p) = (1 - 1.009167^{-60})/.009167 = 45.99$$

To follow the formula watch the keystrokes below:

▌[MAIN]	FIN	TVM	OTHER	12	P/YR	END	[EXIT]
N	I%YR	PV	PMT		FV		
60	11	?	−1		0		
		=45.99					

and make out a short schedule as below:

60		PV =	45.99	--> [STO]	0	
48 [N]		PV =	38.69	--> [STO] [+]	0	
36 [N]		PV =	30.54	--> [STO] [+]	0	
24 [N]		PV =	21.46	--> [STO] [+]	0	
12 [N]		PV =	11.31	--> [STO] [+]	0	
				[RCL]	0	= 148.00

(retain [STO 0] as this factor will be used again later)

As there were 5 (years of) constant lifts (CL) multiply by 5:

```
148 [x] 5 = 740.00   [STO 1]
```

Assuming the calculator has not been cleared:

$$\frac{7000 + 740}{a\underline{\quad\quad}\atop 300|} = \text{pmts}$$

```
7000 [+] [RCL 1] [=]  7,740.00
```

N	I%YR	PV	PMT	FV
300	11	−7740	?	0
			=75.86	

```
Thus the payments for the 6th year onward are £75.86 and therefore:
£75.86 − £5.00  = £70.86  payments year 5  (losing  5 each year)
£70.86 − £5.00  = £65.86      "        "   4
£65.86 − £5.00  = £60.86      "        "   3
£60.86 − £5.00  = £55.86      "        "   2
£55.86 − £5.00  = £50.86      "        "   1
```

(Rounding of the payments to £/p will not affect the APR (11.5%) as can be seen if a DCF calculation is employed.)

The   loan outstanding (LOS) can easily be found for all periods after the end of the 5th year by working backwards from the final year, 300 − (6 x 12) = 228 months to run:

N	I%YR	PV	PMT	FV
228	11	−7740.00	75.86	?
		(RND)	= 3,986.10 LOS_{24}	(end 24th year)

Finding the intermediate balances *before* the end of the 5th year will involve working through each years' balances. For instance, find the balance at the end of the 22nd month:

N	I%YR	PV	PMT	FV
12	11	−7000	50.86	?
				= 7,167.98 [+/−]

N	I%YR	PV	PMT	FV
10	11	−7167.98	55.86	?
				= 7,270.61 LOS$_{22}$

If the structure of the above loan was changed from a £5 lift every year to £80 payments in the last 20 years life of the loan, how can we find the payments for each of the first five years, assuming that the lift is constant?

In this case the formula is:

$$\frac{80a_{\overline{300}|} - 7,000.00}{(a_{\overline{60}|} + a_{\overline{48}|} + a_{\overline{36}|} + a_{\overline{24}|} + a_{\overline{12}|})} = \text{the difference}$$

It will be seen, from the previous example, that the denominator has already been calculated and stored in register 0, so [RCL 0] and 148.00 will display.

N	I%YR	PV	PMT	FV	
300	11	?	−80	0	PV = 8,162.32

$(8,162.32 - 7,000)$ [÷] [RCL] 0] $= 7.85$ "the difference"

The 5th year therefore will have payments of £80 − 7.85 = 72.15 and so on, deducting £7.85 each year....

Specific payments (non-constant)

Sometimes, instead of constant lifts there are specific payments at certain years and the only way of obtaining the correct periodic interest rate is by a DCF calculation.

Assume you wish to quote the APR of a 25 year £10,000 loan with the payments following. Employing the [CFLO] discipline will find a monthly interest rate of .917313%, providing a nominal rate of 11.007758% and consequently an APR of 11.5%.

```
Year 1   payments  £ 50.00 (remember a year has 12 months!)
     2      "      £ 80.00
     3      "      £100.00
     4    onward   £108.00 (namely 300-36 months = 264 "times")
```

Employing these values find the balance at the end of the 16th month:

With .917313189 on display x 12 = 11.01 press I%YR

N	I%YR	PV	PMT	FV
12	11.01	−10000	50	?
				= 10,526.83 [+/−]

N	I%YR	PV	PMT	FV
16−12		−10,526.83	80	?
				= 10,594.00 LOS$_{16}$

CHAPTER 5

Savings and Sinking Funds

General
The normal method, for repayment loans, is for payments to be made in arrears at the end of the year or month. Where savings are concerned, however, in order to obtain the most interest, deposits are usually made at the beginning of the compounding period. These are payments in advance, calculated as savings due.

Deposits made at the [END] of the compounding period, savings ordinary, are sometimes called "sinking funds", as opposed to savings.

Savings DUE (begin mode)
£100 saved each year for two years at 10% interest provides a future value of:

```
£100         x 1.10 = 110.00   end of year 1
(100 + 110) x 1.10 = 231.00   end of year 2
```

Savings ORD (end mode) (Sinking Funds)
Whereas taking the same example:

```
£100                   = 100 deposit at end of year (1)
(100 x 1.10) + 100     = 210 FV      "   "    "    "   (2)
```

Check this on the HP [FIN] [TVM] discipline:

N	I%YR	PV	PMT	FV	OTHER 1	P/YR	BEG	[EXIT]
2	10	0	−100	?				
				= 231.00	OTHER	END		[EXIT]
				?				
				= 210.00				

The actuarial formulae and signs

$$\frac{(1 + i/p)^{np} - 1}{i/p} \times (1 + i/p) = \text{Savings DUE factor} = \overline{s}\underline{\quad}_{np\,|}$$
$$[BEG]$$

$$\frac{(1 + i/p)^{np} - 1}{i/p} = \text{Savings ORD factor} = s\underline{\quad}_{np\,|}$$
$$[END]$$

The actuarial signs for savings due, [BEG], (s with a bar over) and sinking funds, [END], shown above will be employed in the various examples which follow.

Divide the factor found from the equation above into the total amount required at the end of the term and the result will be the necessary deposits to be made per period: alternatively multiply the factor by the periodic payments to provide the future value.

Balances
The balances of deposits made at the beginning or end of a compounding period (with or without an existing balance), or withdrawals from an existing balance, can be found by pressing the [FV] key. Do *not* use the [AMRT] discipline, for this is relevant only to the amortisation of repayment loans and is *not* applicable to savings requirements.

If the discounted cash flow discipline, [CFLO], is employed and the deposits are made at the beginning of the compounding periods, the Net Future Value [NFV] must be multiplied by $(1 + i/p)$ to find the correct final balance. For the convention in DCF calculations, and consequently in the [CFLO] discipline, is to assume that all payments are made in arrears.

Employing the HP cash flow sign convention
Your account at the bank has a healthy credit balance of £10,000 and consequently you decide to withdraw £500 a month for 2 years. Assuming the bank gives interest, at 10% nominal, each month on credit balances held to your name what is your balance at the beginning of the third year?

N	I%YR	PV	PMT	FV	OTHER	12 P/YR	BEG	[EXIT]
24	10	−10000	500	?				

```
                                = −1,129.74 Balance end year 2.
The £10,000.00 is negative because it is not in your pocket
The £    500.00 "  positive because it is     in your pocket
The £ 1,129.74 "  negative because you are overdrawn!
```

Interest/payment periods

If the intervals at which the bank calculates interest do not coincide with the payments periods then some adjustment must be made. The tip is, first convert the nominal *interest* rate to its effective, and then reconvert that value to a nominal rate related to the *periodic* [p] payment periods.

Assume you deposit £100 at the beginning each month for two years and that the bank in question provides 16% nominal interest compounded quarterly, what is the balance due [FV] at the end of the term?

```
      ▌ [MAIN]  FIN   ICONV   PER
          NOM%   EFF%    P
           16      ?      4
                 = 16.99
                  ?      12
                 = 15.79 [STO 0]

[EXIT]  [EXIT]  TVM  OTHER  12 P/YR  BEGIN  [EXIT] <--
```

Providing 15.79 remains on display press [INPUT] and [I%YR]

N	I%YR	PV	PMT	FV	OTHER
24	15.79	0	−100	?	

```
                   = 2,837.66
```

The formula/equation is as follows:

$$\frac{(1 + 15.791285/1200)^{24}}{15.791285/1200} \times 1.013159 \times 100 = 2.837.660463$$

Varying deposits

Sometimes deposits do not remain constant during the term. Assume that each payment is made at the beginning of each year and that the commencing deposit is $500 at an interest rate of 10%. But in the third year the rate rises to 12% and the deposits fall to $300. Finally, in the sixth (last) year the deposits are $25 *per month* and the monthly rate is $(15/12)$%. What is the value of the fund at the end of the 6th year?

```
Actuarially the equation is    500s___
                                   2 |   at 10%
                       PLUS     300s___
                                   3 |   at 12%
                       PLUS      25s___
                                  12 |   at 1.25%
```

and the keystrokes are:

```
[EXIT]   FIN   TVM  1 P/YR  BEGIN   [EXIT]
   N     I%YR   PV     PMT    FV
   2      10     0    -500    ? = 1,155.00 [+/-]
   N     I%YR   PV     PMT    FV
   3      12   -1155  -300    ? = 2,756.49 [+/-]
   N     I%YR   PV     PMT    FV
  12     1.25 -2756.49 -25    ? = 3,525.14 Balance.
```

Savings with percentage increments

Sometimes savings plans, notably insurance contracts, increase the deposit requirements by so much each year, often by an annual percentage lift – even if payments are monthly.

For example assuming a 10 years term at 10% annual rate with a 6% uplift on the payments each year and a required future value of £10,000. What is the first deposit required – and the payments in each subsequent year?

The following two programs will provide both the initial payment necessary to meet a required future value, with each subsequent payment being increased either annually or periodically, or the future value derived from a number of increment payments.

Key in the following progams **SAVINGS/INCR * *** and **SAVINGS/INCR/LIFT**

```
SAVINGS/INCR:IF(S(FV) OR S(PMTS):RND(FV÷(
USPV(RATE%÷P:P)x(RATE%÷P÷100+1)xSPFV(INCR
:ΣYRS)xUSFV(((RATE%÷P÷100+1)^P÷(INCR÷10
0+1)-1)x100:ΣYRS)xSPFV(RATE%÷P:P)xSPPV(
INCR:1)):FIX)-PMTS:(FV÷(1+(RATE%÷P÷100))^
(ΣYRSxP)))-PV
```

(Ensure a space before/after OR above)

| FV | RATE% | P | INCR | ΣYRS | MORE |
| FIX | PMTS | PV | | | MORE |

The program assumes payments in advance. Zero must be retained at all times in [PV] except when finding the [PV].

```
SAVINGS/INCR/LIFT:SGN(ΣYRS)xRND(PMTSx((IN
CR÷100+1)^IF(#?>ΣYRS:INV(0):(#?-1))):FIX)
=NEXT
```

| ΣYRS | PMTS | INCR | #? | FIX | NEXT |

Taking the above example, namely a future bank balance of £10,000.00 required at the end of 10 years. With the bank giving 10% nominal interest, with an annual 6% percentage lift each year, what is the first annual payment and the first monthly payments?

[EXIT]	↓↑	SAVINGS/INCR	CALC		
FV	RATE%	P	INCR	ΣYRS	MORE
10000	10	1	6	10	
FIX	PMTS	PV			MORE
2	?	0	(to find PMTS 0 *must* be input to PV)		
	= 452.91	(pmts in advance)			

and for a sinking fund, payments in arrears:

With 452.91 on display: [+] MORE [RCL] RATE% [%] [=] 498.20
pmts in arrears

For monthly payments:

```
[INPUT] 12 to   P    and press   PMTS =  38.52 in advance
[RCL] RATE% [÷] 1200 [+] 1 [x] ▌ LAST =  38.84 in arrears
```

Reverting to the annual payments, 1 input to [P] and repress [PMTS] = 452.91. What is your last, 10th year, deposit?

```
[EXIT]   ↓↑  SAVINGS/INCR/LIFT    CALC
  ΣYRS    PMTS      INCR    #?    FIX    NEXT
   10    452.9100     6      10    2      ?
```
$$= 765.18 \ PMT_{10}$$

This is the type of calculation where a schedule is useful to see exactly "what happens to the money":

Schedule for Savings DUE:

452.91	x 1.10	=	498.20	1
498.20 + (452.91 x 1.06^1)	x 1.10	=	1,076.11	2
1,076.11 + (452.91 x 1.06^2)	x 1.10	=	1,743.50	3
1,743.50 + (452.91 x 1.06^3)	x 1.10	=	2,511.22	4
2,511.22 + (452.91 x 1.06^4)	x 1.10	=	3,391.31	5
3,391.31 + (452.91 x 1.06^5)	x 1.10	=	4,397.14	6
4,397.14 + (452.91 x 1.06^6)	x 1.10	=	5,543.57	7
5,543.57 + (452.91 x 1.06^7)	x 1.10	=	6,847.03	8
6,847.03 + (452.91 x 1.06^8)	x 1.10	=	8,325.79	9
8,325.79 + (452.91 x 1.06^9)	x 1.10	=	10,000.07	10

Schedule for savings ORD: (sinking funds)

(498.20 x 1.10)		=	548.02	1
(548.02 x ") + (492.20 x 1.06)		=	1,076.11	2
(1,076.11 x ") + (528.09 x 1.06)		=	1,743.50	3
~ ~ ~ ~ ~ ~ ~ ~ ~ ~ ~ ~ ~ ~ ~ ~ ~ ~		~ ~ ~ ~ ~ ~ ~ ~ ~	
(6,847.03 x ") + (749.11 x 1.06)		=	8,325.79	9
(8,325.79 x ") + 841.70		=	10,000.05	10

First the conventional formula:

$$\frac{FV \times (1 + j)^{-n}}{\overline{s}_{\overline{n}|} \text{ at } f\%} = \text{1st payment}$$

where i = commencing annual interest rate as a decimal (.100000)
    j = the annual percentage increment as a decimal (.060000)
    f = [(1 + i)/(1 + j)] − 1   (.037736)

$$\frac{10,000.00}{\frac{(1.03774^{10} - 1)}{0.03774} \times 1.03774 \times 1.06^{10}} = \text{£452.91 1st pmt DUE}$$

Monthly calculations with an annual percentage uplift
Above it was seen that the payments were annual, the 6% increment also being an annual lift, consequently, for monthly payments, the "j" factor must be calculated slightly differently: $((1 + 10/1200)^{12})/1.06) = 1.042182$ and this replaces the previous factor in the above formula.

$$\frac{FV}{\ddot{a}_{\overline{p}|} \text{ [at } i/p\%] \times (1 + j)^n \times \overline{s}_{\overline{n}|} \text{ [at } f\%]} = \text{first periodic deposit}$$

$$\frac{10,000.00}{\frac{(1- 1.008333^{-12})}{.008333} \times 1.00833 \times 1.06^{10} \times \frac{(1.042182^{10} - 1)}{.042182} \times 1.042182}$$

$$= £10,000 \div 259.62 \qquad = £38.52$$

Example: You want save around £2,000 at the end of two years. Your bank manager tells you that he will give you 12% nominal, with interest calculated monthly. You ask him how much would you need to deposit *monthly* to achieve this. After a slight hesitation he replies "£73.41, providing you make your deposits at the beginning of each month." "Alternatively," he continues, "if you prefer, you can start off the first year with £70 monthly deposits and then increase the monthly deposits to £77 next year."

Is your bank manager right? If you act on his alternative recommendation what will your balance be at the end of two years?

```
[EXIT]    ↓↑   SAVINGS/INCR   CALC
   FV    RATE%    P     INCR    ΣYRS    MORE
  2000    12      12     0       2
  FIX    PMTS    PV
   2       ?      0   (don't forget the 0)
             = 73.41 per month


   FV    RATE%    P     INCR    ΣYRS    MORE
   ?                    10
  = 1,996.69
  FIX    PMTS    PV
   11     70      0   (don't forget the 11 FIX)
```

The increment rate of 10% resulted, of course, from the bank manager's suggestion of £70, followed by £77, payments monthly: $77/70 - 1 \times 100 = 10\%$

What would be the final balance if you decided to start with £70 but to pay £78 for the last 12 months? Try a DCF calculation:

```
▌ [MAIN]   FIN   CFLO   ▌ [CLEAR DATA] CLEAR THE LIST?   YES

FLOW(0)=?   0 [INPUT]  FLOW(1)=? 70 [INPUT]  #TIMES(1)=1 12 [INPUT]
                       FLOW(2)=? 78 [INPUT]  #TIMES(2)=1 12 [INPUT]
[EXIT]   CALC 1 press   I%   press   NFV    =  1,989.60
and because pmts are in advance [x] 1.01 [=] 2,009.50 FV
```

Now check on the program. . .

```
▌ EXIT]   SOLVE  ↓↑ SAVINGS/INCR   CALC
   78 [÷] 70 [–] 1 [x] 100 [=] 11.428571 press   INCR
    FV    RATE%    P     INCR       ΣYRS    MORE
    ?      12      12   11.428571    2
   = 2,009.50
   FIX    PMTS    PV
   11     70       0
```

Example: (from an HP-12C *Solutions Book*): "Today you deposit $1,000 into a savings account that earns 9½% interest, compounded annually. Each year you plan to increase the amount of your deposit by 15%. How much will you accumulate in 20 years?"

FV	RATE%	P	INCR	ΣYRS	MORE
?	9.50	1	15	20	
= 203,568.97					

FIX	PMTS	PV
11	1000	0

Example: (from the HP-17/19 *Owner's Manuals*), related to an American style Taxable Retirement Account: "If you invest $3,000 each year for 35 years, with dividends taxed as ordinary income, how much will you have in your account at retirement? Assume an annual dividend rate of 8.175% and a tax rate of 28%, and that payments begin today. What will be the purchasing power of that amount in today's dollars, assuming 8% annual inflation?"

The net rate of interest will be:
8.175 x (100 – 28)/100 = 8.175 x .72 = 5.8860%

FV	RATE%	P	INCR	ΣYRS	MORE
?	5.886	1	0	35	
= 345,505.61					

FIX	PMTS	PV
11	3000	0

and discounting the 8% inflation factor:

FV	RATE%	P	INCR	ΣYRS	MORE
	8				

FIX	PMTS	PV
		?
		= 23,368.11

Periodic percentage increments

Very occasionally the percentage increases relate to the periodic payments. Monthly increments to monthly payments would be unlikely, but with semi–annual instalments a depositor might care to increase each deposit. Assume a £10,000 required balance from 10% nominal, after 2 years of semi–annual deposits, with a 3% lift every six months. What is the first payment necessary?

The existing formula/program can be used for semi–annual increments, providing the following input method is employed Halve the rates and double the years, for this method suits the format of the provided program – and consequently avoids the need for yet another program.

FV	RATE%	P	INCR	ΣYRS	MORE
10000	5	1	3	4	

FIX	PMTS	PV			MORE
2	?	0			

                  =2,116.46 [+] [RCL] RATE% [%] [=] 2,222.29 pmts in arrears

```
2,116.46                              x 1.05  =  2,222.29
2,222.29 + (2,116.46 x 1.03^1)        x 1.05  =  4,622.35
4,622.35 + (2,116.46 x 1.03^2)        x 1.05  =  7,211.09
7,211.09 + (2,116.46 x 1.03^3)        x 1.05  =  9,999.99   QED.
```

CHAPTER 6

UK Building Society Mortgage Calculations

UK building society methods
The building societies require monthly repayments of capital and interest but, ignoring more conventional methods which make up the balances at the end of each month, building societies calculate their payments annually. These annual payments are then divided by 12 to determine the monthly payments – suitably rounded upward – and reconciliation occurs at the end of each year, when the annual days' interest due is compared with the amount derived from the total number of payments made.

A £25,000 loan over 25 years at 13% nominal would require £284.25 payments each year. Building societies calculate all their scale payments per £1,000 and so:

$$1,000/(1 - (1.13^- 25))/.13 = £136.43$$

These annual payments, divided by 12 and rounded upward to the nearest penny, provide the monthly payments per the basic £1,000, and thus, in the case of a £25,000 loan the £11.37 is multiplied by 25 to give £284.25 [STO 0].

And employing the HP [FIN] [TVM] discipline:

FIN	TVM	OTHER 1	P/Y	END	[EXIT] ▌ [CLEAR DATA]
N	I%YR	PV	PMTS	FV	
25	13	−1000	?	0	

= 136.43

and 136.43 [÷] 12 [=] 11.368827 rounded to 11.37 [x] 25 [=] £284.25

Please note that the four programs used for building society calculations are to be found on page 78 at the end of this chapter.

Disclosure
In 1985 a new finance act regularised the narrowing gap between banking and building societies' method of conducting business. Banks, much to their annoyance, were in future to conform to the long established practice of building societies, which repay interest to their lenders net of tax. Building societies, to their equal annoyance, were no longer exempt from disclosing the Annual Percentage Rate of Charge (APR) and the Total Amount Paid (TAP).

But complications arose, for it was realised that, since payments are always in arrears, if an advance was made during the month of December there would be no payment to offset the interest between the date of the advance and the year end. In such a case the quoted term might well be understated – and if so illegal.

Sticking to the previous example, an advertised building society £25,000 mortgage at 13%, over 25 years, with payments of £284.25 monthly. If the loan was advanced on (say) December 1 then at reconciliation on December 31 the balance of the loan, for the next 300 months, would stand at:

13 [÷] 100 [x] 31 [÷] 365 [+] 1 [x] 25,000 [=] £25,276.03
                                         year end balance

Incidentally, it is thirty-*one* days' interest because building societies require the "days to and from two dates" method, namely "days between" plus one day.

The reason why this complication could cause an illegal disclosure is that *all* the quoted information must be correct, and if the quoted rate of 13% is correct a December advance would make the "term" of 25 years incorrect.

Taking the monthly payment above, "annualised", namely (£284.25 x 12 = £3,411) enter this and other values below:

N	I%YR	PV	PMT	FV
?	13	25,276.03	–3,411	0	(don't forget the 0)

= 27.05 (years), against a "quoted" term of 25 years!

The "excess"

Assuming that the above loan was advanced on February 1 it will be found that there are 333 days between the advance date and the year end and therefore 334 interest days (to conform to the societies' methods), and 10 payment periods to the year end (March-December); therefore, on a loan of £25,000 at 13% over 25 years, the *LOS*, the loan outstanding, at the first reconciliation is:

```
[25,000 x (1 + (.13 x 334/365))] - (284.25 x 10) = £25,131.47
```

an excess of £131.47 which can best be found by employing the BS/VALUES program:

```
█ [MAIN]   SOLVE    ↓↑   BS/VALUES       CALC
   LOAN    NOM%   DAYS    MTHS   FEES    MORE
   25000     13    334      10      0
    PV     PMTS    LOS                   MORE
     0    284.25    ?   = -131.47 excess
    PV     PMTS    LOS                   MORE
  -25000  284.25    ?   = -25,131.47 balance
```

The accrued interest

The Building Societies Association decided that the best method to overcome this problem of possibly illegal quotations was to insist that borrowers should repay the accrued interest (a/i), due between advance and first reconciliation, at the time of the advance.

Before the necessity of repaying the a/i arose everyone knew that the balance at the first year end was loan plus days' interest less any payments made (as outlined above), but few knew, or were required to know, the precise interest engendered. So what exactly is the accrued interest, how does it arise and how is it calculated?

Scale payments are calculated assuming twelve repayments per year; but in the year of the advance, as payments are in arrears, there cannot possibly be more than eleven. Furthermore it must be remembered that the monthly repayments contain proportions of both interest and of capital.

To find the accrued interest calculate as follows:

```
(25,000 x .13 x 334/365) − (25,000 x .13 x 10/12) = £265.64 (a/i)
(    daily interest    ) − (  monthly interest  ) = (accrued)
 25,000 x .13 x ((334 x 12/365)−10) ÷ 12            = £265.64
```

Employing the BS/VALUES program:

LOAN	NOM%	DAYS	MTHS	FEES	MORE
25000	13	334	10	0	

PV	PMTS	LOS			MORE
?					

```
= −24,734.36 and [+] 25,000 [=] 265.64 a/i
```

Consequently the loan outstanding at the end of the first year's reconciliation is loan plus days interest *less* any payments made, *less* the accrued interest, *less* any front-end fees: £25,131.47 − 265.64 = £24,865.83

LOAN	NOM%	DAYS	MTHS	FEES	MORE
25000	13	334	10	0	

PV	PMTS	LOS			MORE
−24734.36	284.25	?			

```
= −24,865.83
```

The amount of excess and front-end fees can be found by keeping [LOS] on display and pressing −[RCL PV] = −131.47 with fees of (say) £150 the answer would become −281.47.

Disclosure − requirements for quotations
There are two distinct requirements, the APR and TAP, for either a "general" quotation or a "specific" quotation involving detailed disussion of a particular mortgage.

Every society must decide when the first repayment is to be made, for this dictates much of the resulting calculation. Some require all repayments to be made on the same day of the month as the advance date, others favour the first calendar day of each month. Consequently the method employed will affect the date of the first payment after the advance, and thus the effective rate of interest charged over the whole period.

If the method is to require payments to be made on the first day of each month then the first repayment is made on the first day of the month after the advance, providing the advance is made within the first three quarters of the month concerned – if not payment is postponed until the first day of the month following.

In the first case, for a general disclosure, the average is considered to be half a month (factor .5, see below), whereas in the latter case the average is assumed to be 3/4 of a month (factor .75, see below). Other variations might be a whole month's interest required for the month in which the advance was made, irrespective of the actual date of the advance, or even, in some cases, a month and a half's interest. In those cases the factor is 1 or 1.5 respectively for general disclosure.

Whichever method is employed for determining the first repayment in the specific quotation *must* also apply to a general quotation. In other words, if the current method of a particular building society requires a complete month's interest for the month in which the advance was made (factor 1) then not only will this method be applied to the specific quotation but it must also apply to general quotations.

Front-end fees
In the same way front-end fees, legal and search fees, etc, must be considered for disclosure. If a society *always* makes certain charges then these must be deducted from the loan (less a/i) before the calculation is made to determine the periodic rate for the general disclosure.

Disclosure – general quotation
Taking a £25,000 loan at 13% nominal over a period of 25 years with monthly scale payments of £284.25, and assuming that the society concerned requires a "first of the month" payment (factor 0.75), the general quote APR will be:

▌[MAIN]	SOLVE ↑↓	BS/VALUES	CALC		
LOAN	NOM%	DAYS	MTHS	FEES	MORE
25000	13	0	−.75	0	
PV	PMTS	LOS			MORE

? = −24,796.88 (note the −.75 negative factor input)

Or by calculation:

```
RND(25,000 x .13 x .75 ÷ 12) - 25,000  =  -24,796.87
```

The rounding is necessary because the notional a/i paid is, notionally, cash across the counter at the notional advance.

```
▌ [MAIN]   FIN    TVM   OTHER   12  P/YR    END    [EXIT] <--
[INPUT]  -24,796.87 on display press   PV   and input data:
    N       I%YR     PV      PMT        FV
   300       ?   -24796.87 284.25       0
            = 13.244890 (nom%)
            = 14.079261 (eff%)
            = 14.0      (APR%)
```

Disclosure – specific quotation

The only difference to the above is that for a specific quotation the precise date of the advance is known and from that premise the APR and TAP calculations are determined. Taking the above example, assume that the advance is made on February 1 which requires 334 interest days between the advance date and the first year end reconciliation. We know from a previous section that the accrued interest is £265.64

Taking the specific quotation example above, the value is loan – a/i – fees (here £150): £25,000 - 265.64 - 150 = £24,584.36

```
▌ [MAIN] SOLVE  ↑↓ BS/VALUES  CALC   input above data
   LOAN    NOM%   DAYS   MTHS   FEES   MORE
  25000     13    334     10     150
    PV     PMT    LOS                  MORE
     ?
    = -24,584.36
```

```
▌ [MAIN]   FIN    TVM   OTHER   1 P/YR    END    [EXIT] <--
-24,584.36  on  display  [INPUT] press    PV
    N       I%YR     PV      PMT      FV
   300       ?   -24584.36 284.25     0   (don't forget the 0)
            =  1.114649 (x 12 = 13.375792)
```

To find the effective rate, with 13.375792 on display:

```
[EXIT] ICONV   PER    press  NOM%
 NOM%   EFF%    P
13.38    ?      12    = 14.227050  (Eff%)
                      = 14.2       (APR%)
```

Total Amount Paid (TAP)

The total amount paid is the total amount of the payments made *plus* the a/i, *plus* any front-end fees. In this example the accrued is £265.64 and the fees are £150, together £415.64. Thes front-end amount being found from the loan amount less the present value £25,000 – 24,584.36 = £415.64

Consequently the TAP is:
```
(Pmts   x  n ) +    accrued + fees
                 ( loan  –   PV   )
(284.25 x 300) + (25,000 – 24,584.36) = £85,690.64 TAP
```

The BS/TAP program was designed for more complex calculations (see later), but the second part, with some mental adjustment, can be used in this instance – perhaps as a check on manual working.

The program finds the front-end values by subtracting the PV from the loan amount; to save time, and in order to circumvent the program format, key-in the front-end fees and press [LOAN]:

```
▌ [MAIN] SOLVE   ↓↑  BS/TAP           CALC
    N      FV    PMTS  NOM%   MTHS    MORE
    0      0    284.25    0      0
   NP    LOAN    PV    LAST    TAP    MORE
   300  415.64    0      0       ?
                                   =85,690.64
```

Maximum Advance Scheme (MAS)

This scheme is merely the accrued interest by another name. A simplified method employed by some societies to cover, without detailed explanation, the necessity for borrowers to pay the front-end accrued interest contribution!

Endowment loans

The repayments for endowment loans are interest only, the capital sum being repaid at maturity. The above calculations for the accrued interest and disclosure obtain and there is no need for the precise last payment method (see below).

Taking a loan of £25,000 over 25 years, advanced February 1, with a nominal rate of 13.50%, and employing the program, BS/VALUES, find the value (cost less accrued):

```
█ [MAIN]   ↓↑  BS/VALUES       CALC
    LOAN        NOM%     DAYS      MTHS     FEES     MORE
    25000       13.50    334       10       0
     PV         PMTS     LOS                         MORE
     ?
      = -24,724.14 [STO 1]
     PV         PMTS     LOS                         MORE
 -24,724.14      ?      -25000
               = 281.25 [STO 0]


█ [MAIN]    FIN      TVM      OTHER 12 P/YR    END    [EXIT]
     N        I%YR     PV       PMT       FV
    300        ?      [RCL1]   [RCL0]    25000 (endowment)
             = 13.655916 (nom%)  14.542 (eff%) 14.5% (APR%)
```

The TAP is:
```
(281.25 x 300) + (25,000 - 24,724.14) (which = 275.86) plus fees, if
any, plus loan = £109,650.86
```

The disclosure requirements, when originally conceived, were never intended to relate to mortgage loans such as this; consequently, although correct and indeed a legal requirement for disclosure, the TAP is both unrealistic and misleading!

Endowment loans always have the addition of an insurance policy, the cost of which may have to be included as a front-end fee for APR and TAP disclosure. Each society is advised by its own legal department as to whether to include or not; societies usually cover such costs by raising the interest rate for endowment loans – by (say) half a point.

A refinement – the "last payment"

And now for the bad news! While the above method of finding the APR and the TAP, for either a general or specific quotation, is generally accepted as the conventional method for disclosure, a few elegant building societies have some reservations and prefer a yet more detailed approach. Namely the calculating of the amount of the last payment prior to finding the APR and TAP – irrespective of the fact that few, if any, home loans ever run the full term or that the quoted rate is unlikely to remain unchanged over the full term!

While other societies give little credence to this "precise" method it must be accepted as the ideal, although the APR differs in no way from the conventional method and the TAP is only a few hundreds less – a minor saving which is unlikely to prevent the inevitable cardiac arrest suffered by any first time borrower. This method does give accurate, rather than greatly inflated, values for the TAP when the payments, for some reason, are greater than the scale payments – as will be seen in the second of the examples that follow.

First the exact number of period payments due must be determined; then the balance at the end of that term; then the exact amount of the last payment. The calculation is complex, and in reality is more suitable to a full computer program rather than to a formula-based program. Nevertheless, the "precise" and correct APR and TAP can be found using the three programs below, complex and irritating though the constant switching of programs will be.

The calculation of APR and TAP

Still using the example of a loan of £25,000 over a term of 25 years at 13% with monthly payments of £284.25 [STO 0], the accrued interest was determined as £265.64. Assume fees of £150 and that the loan was advanced February 1 giving 334 interest days to the year end reconciliation day, and 10 monthly payments of £284.25 during that time.

Employing the BS/VALUES program find the [PV] and the balance of the loan, [LOS], at the first year end reconciliation:

LOAN	NOM%	DAYS	MTHS	FEES	MORE
25000	13	334	10	150	

PV	PMTS	LOS			MORE
?	284.25	?			
= −24,584.36		= −24.865.83			
[STO 1]		[STO 2]			

The loan outstanding £24,865.83 consists of the loan, £25,000, *plus* the excess of £131,47, *less* the accrued interest of £265.64. It is this value which is used to find the last payment. The fee is applicable only to the APR and TAP *not* the [LOS].

Employing the BS/LAST program, first find the FV. The previous data will be in situ as the values are shared with the previous program. The only value, therefore, to be input is [N] and, assuming an annual perspective, input the full term (here 25) and press [FV].

The object is to find a *positive* FV, so if the first attempt is unsuccessful continue to reduce the term by 1 year. When a positive [FV] is found press [LAST] to find the last payment:

▌ [MAIN]	SOLVE	↓↑	BS/LAST	CALC

N	NOM%	LOS	PMTS	FV	LAST
25				?	
				=−2,903.25	

N	NOM%	LOS	PMTS	FV	LAST
24				?	
				= 449.34	? = 174.82 [STO 4]

Now the APR and the TAP must be found. First, therefore, it is necessary to find the exact number of payments made during the loan term, remembering that there were 10 months from advance to first year end. The TAP program will find both the TAP *and* the correct number of payments so that the APR can later be found on the [TVM] discipline.

Coming from both BS/VALUE and BS/LAST, the BS/TAP program will have all the shared values in situ except for label [FRNT], which can be filled by [RCL 1] – the loan amount:

```
[EXIT]  ↓↑  TAP  CALC
    N       FV      PMTS   NOM%   MTHS  MORE
  (24)  (449.34) (284.25) (13)   (10)
   NP   LOAN      PV     LAST   TAP   MORE
    ? = 299 = total number of payments made
```

The TAP is the payments times the number of payments plus the a/i, plus any fees, plus the last payment. The program, in this example, found that there were 299 period payments, and so the TAP becomes:

```
 N  x  Pmts   +           PV      +  Loan   +  Last pmt =    TAP
299 x [RCL 0] [+] [(] [RCL PV] [+] 25000 [+] [RCL 4] [=] 85,581.21
299 x 284.25  +     (-24,584.36  +  25000) + 174.82 =       "
```

The [FRNT] value, which must be input, is the front-end payments, namely the accrued interest and fees, if any.

This is found by [RCL 1] (–24,584.36) + loan (25,000) = £415.64 (being the a/i, £265.64 + the fees, £150) – and using the second part of the above program:

```
    NP     LOAN       PV       LAST     TAP
  (299)  (25000) (-24584.36) (174.82)   ? = 85,581.21 TAP
```

The APR is found by switching to the HP TVM program:

```
[EXIT] [EXIT]  FIN   TVM  1 P/YR  END  MODE
    N    I%YR    PV    PMT      FV
  299     ?    [RCL1] [RCL0]  [RCL4]
          =  1.114449 x 12
          = 13.373392 (nom%)
          = 14.224339 (eff%)        = 14.2% (APR%)
```

Consequently the APR is 14.2% and the TAP £85,581.21 and readers may care to compare the "specific quotation" example above, namely an effective rate of 14.227054 (the APR% being the same as above) and a TAP of £85,690.64.

Example: A building society (repayment) loan of £57,000 at
15.125% over a term of 25 years with monthly payments of
£741.57 [STO 0]. There is a front-end fee of £384.45. The odd
days' interest at the end of the term should be treated as one
month's interest. The advance date, and the factors, 334 days
and 10 months, being the same as in the previous example

▌ [MAIN] SOLVE ↓↑ BS/VALUES   CALC   input above data

LOAN	NOM%	DAYS	MTHS	FEES	MORE
57000	15.125	334	10	384.45	

PV			PMTS	LOS	
?			741.57	?	
= −55,910.89 [STO1]				= −56,768.67 [STO2]	

▌ [MAIN] SOLVE   ↓↑ BS/LAST CALC

N	NOM%	LOS	PMTS	FV		LAST
23				?		?
				= 6,092.20		= 109.15 [STO 4]

[EXIT]   ↓↑   BS/TAP CALC

N	FV	PMTS	NOM%	MTHS	MORE
(23)	(6092.20)	(741.57)	(15.125)	(10)	

NP	LOAN	PV	LAST	TAP	MORE
?	(57000)	(−55910.89)	(109.15)	?	
=295				= 219,961.41 TAP	

The TAP is some £3,500 less than if calculated by conventional means.

[EXIT] [EXIT]   FIN   TVM   1 P/YR END MODE

N	I%YR	PV	PMT	FV	OTHER
295	?	[RCL1]	[RCL0]	[RCL4]	
		−55,910.89	741.57	109.15	

                   = 1.296753% monthly
          x 12 = 15.561031% nominal   Convert to effective:
                  = 16.720267% effective
                  = 16.7% APR

*A further detailed examination of building Society methods and
the above somewhat complex "last payment" calculations can be
found in* Financial Calculations for Business *(unrelated to
any particular calculator) by the author and also published by
Kogan Page.*

Mortgage Interest Relief at Source (MIRAS)

The tax relief on home loans is at the basic rate of tax subject to the capital value not being greater than £30,000 (1988). For loans above £30,000 the rebate is allowed on the first £30,000 only – the remainder receiving no further relief.

The borrower of a home loan repays both capital and interest, the annual interest being nominally income to the societies and thus subject to tax. Each borrower, whose payments are reported to the revenue, is given relief at the basic rate of tax. Should the borrower be subject to a higher rate appropriate adjustments will be made later.

This apparently somewhat unwieldy method has worked reasonably well for years, but delays in sorting out the correct claw-back sometimes occur, which can be inconvenient for the borrower and doubtless tiresome for the Revenue.

As a result an option was provided a few years ago whereby borrowers, instead of making gross payments and in due course having the tax rebate returned, could if they wished make net payments, the interest in effect being net of tax thus precluding any further Revenue interference – except for those whose personal tax is higher than the basic rate!
As readers will be aware this scheme is called Mortgage Interest Relief at Source, or MIRAS for short, and the method treats the nominal rate as net of tax. Assuming that the basic rate of tax was 25% then instead of the asking rate being 13% the net rate would be 13 x .75 = 9.75 per cent. Over 25 years for a loan of £1,000 the monthly payments would reduce from £11.37 gross to £9.00 net, or, on £25,000, from £284.25 to £225.00.

The Inland Revenue make it quite clear, however, that the fact that MIRAS appears to result in lower interest rates to the borrower cannot be allowed to create the illusion of a reduced effective rate. Therefore, even if the borrower has opted for MIRAS, the calculations for disclosure *must* be assessed on the *gross* nominal interest rate, on the *gross* monthly payments, and the *gross* a/i.

As relief is currently limited to £30,000 any loan above that amount was not MIRAS calculated prior to 1987. But from 1987 societies were able to accept "constant" payment contracts whereby part of the payments could be considered as tax relief-ed, the remaining part not so. The constant payments required by societies are not Revenue sponsored, it remains the responsibility of the individual societies to remit the correct tax to the authorities.

The calculation of constant payments

How are the constant payments to be calculated? The short answer is, not without difficulty! The trick is, first, to determine, by interpolation, the cross-over point (in years or months) where the different net/gross payments would notionally change if the payments were not constant.

For example, for a loan of £50,000 at 11% nominal over a term of 25 years the gross monthly payments would be £495, and if the tax was 25% basic then the net payments would fall to £400.00 – but of course only the first £30,000 is eligible for relief. Consequently, if constant payments are to be made over the whole term they must be calculated in such a way as to allow for the tax rebate only on the first £30,000.

Obviously such payments will fall somewhere between those payments relevant to the net and gross values. The formula below (MIRAS/CONSTANT) is designed first to find the cross-over point and then, with that value as the term, to find the constant payments.

Constant payments formula

The formula outlined below requires the calculation to be
such that both sides of the equation are the same, the
variable being the cross-over factor.

```
Where:  A  = the loan amount
        R  = the relief limit         (at present £30,000)
        i  = the gross interest rate  (as a decimal)
        j  = the net   interest rate  (as a decimal)
        t  = the cross over factor in years (or months optional)
```

Actuarially shown as:

$$\frac{(A - R)}{a_{\overline{t}|} \text{ at } i\%} + [R \times (j)] \quad \text{MUST equal} \quad \frac{R}{a_{\overline{n-t}|} \text{ at } j\%}$$

If the calculations are annually based then both sides of the
equation must finally be divided by 12 to provide *monthly*
payments with the resulting equation being:

$$\frac{\dfrac{(A - R)}{[1 - (1 + i)^{-t}]/i} + [R \times (j)]}{12} = \frac{\dfrac{R}{[1 - (1 + j)^{-(n-t)}]/j}}{12}$$

Unless otherwise stated, in all the examples below the relief
limit is taken as £30,000 with a basic tax level of 25%.

Example: A loan of £50,000 at 11% nominal over 25 years. In this case at a basic rate of 25% and a net rate 8.25% (found from 11 x .75 = 8.25) the cross-over factor, t, is 16.715963, accordingly (n – t) = 25 – 16.715963 = 8.2840

$$\frac{20,000.00}{1 - (1.11^{-16.7160})/.11} + (30,000 \times .0825) \quad \frac{30,000.00}{(1 - 1.0825^{-8.2840})/.0825}$$

	12		12
2,665.81	+ 2,475.00		
	5,140.81/12	=	5,140.81/12
	428.40	=	428.40

Once the two sides of the equation balance the cross-over factor *must* be correct. Thus the 16.625670 years can be considered notionally as 8.4 years at the net rate (for the £30,000) and 16.6 years at the gross rate (for the remaining £20,000 in this example). The cross-over factor is that period which refers to the latter part of the loan, namely the notionally gross period; however once the payments are determined the cross over factor is academic. With the cross-over factor correct the payments, which produced that factor, *must* be the constant payments throughout the whole term of the loan.

Taking the same example, namely a £50,000 loan at 11% over 25 years, at an assumed basic rate of tax of 25%:

[MAIN]	↓↑	MIRAS/CONSTANT		CALC	[DSP] 6	[CLEAR DATA]
LOAN	I%	N	BASIC	XOVER	MORE	
50000	11	25	25	?		
				= 16.715963		
FIX	PMTS				MORE	
6	?	= 428.401174				
2	?	= 428.40 **				

When using the MIRAS/CONSTANT program, because of the fairly complex interpolation required, to assist a rapid response, key-in 0 press [XOVER], key-in .5 press [XOVER], and then RE-press [XOVER].

Examples: Find the monthly payments at the following basic rates:
(a) A loan of £31,000 at 8% nominal over 5 years (30%).
(b) A loan of £230,000 at 20% nominal over 30 years (25%).
(c) A loan of £50,000 at 11% nominal over 25 years (25%)
     if calculated *monthly*, unlike the BS annual methods.

LOAN	I%	N	BASIC	XOVER	MORE
31000	8	5	30	?	

$= 0.186875$

FIX	PMTS				MORE
2	?				

$= 606.88$

LOAN	I%	N	BASIC	XOVER	MORE
230000	20	30	25	?	

$= 29.240706$

FIX	PMTS				MORE
2	?				

$= 3,724.54$

LOAN	I%	N	BASIC	XOVER	MORE
50000	11/12	25x12	25	?	

$= 202.677136$

FIX	PMTS				MORE
11	?				

$= 35.317701 \times 12 = 423.81$ monthly pmt
                                c.f.,** above

Please *not*:

FIX	PMTS	
2	?	$= 35.32 \times 12 = 423.84$

The average advance in the UK (April 1988) from the National Home Loans Corporation PLC was £53,000.

When using the program for banking methods, where payments are calculated monthly, delete 2 in the last line of the MIRAS program. Input nominal rate/12 to the [I%] and years x 12 to the [N] for monthly payments. For quarterly payments for 12 read 4.

Key in the following programs **BS/VALUES * *, BS/LAST, BS/TAP** and **MIRAS/CONSTANT * ***

BS/VALUES:IF(S(LOAN) OR S(PV):RND((LOANxN
OM%÷100xDAYS÷365)-(LOANxNOM%÷100xMTHS÷12)
-LOAN+FEES:2)-PV:RND(PV-((LOANxNOM%÷100xD
AYS÷365)-(PMTSxMTHS)+FEES):2)-LOS)

(Ensure a space before/after OR above)

LOAN	NOM%	DAYS	MTHS	FEES	MORE
PV	PMTS	LOS			MORE

BS/LAST:IF(S(FV OR S(PMTS):(0xNxNOM%xLOSx
PMTSxFV)+LOSxSPFV(NOM%:N)+USFV(NOM%:N)xPM
TSx12+FV:RND(FP((((INT(FV÷PMTS)+1)x(FVxNO
M%÷100)÷12)+FV)÷PMTS)xPMTS:2)-LAST)

(Ensure a space before/after or above)

N	NOM%	LOS	PMTS	FV	LAST

BS/TAP:IF(S(NP) OR S(PMTS):(Nx12)+INT(INT
(((INT(FV÷PMTS)+1)x(FVxNOM%÷100)÷12+FV)÷P
MTS)+MTHS)-NP:RND((NPxPMTS)+LOAN+PV+LAST:
2)-TAP)

(Ensure a space before/after or above)

N	FV	PMTS	NOM%	MTHS	MORE
NP	LOAN	PV	LAST	TAP	MORE

MIRAS/CONSTANT:IF(S(XOVER) OR S(BASIC):(L
OAN-30000)÷USPV(I%:SGN(N)xSGN(BASIC)xXOVE
R)+(30000xI%÷100x(1-BASIC÷100))-(30000÷US
PV(I%x(1-BASIC÷100):N-XOVER)):RND((((LOAN
-30000)÷USPV(I%:XOVER)+(30000xI%÷100x(1-B
ASIC÷100)))÷12):FIX)-PMTS)

(Ensure a space before/after or above)

LOAN	I%	N	BASIC	XOVER	MORE
FIX	PMTS				MORE

If the present £30,000 tax relief limit is altered, adjust the
values in the above program accordingly.

CHAPTER 7

Hire Purchase and Leasing

The differences between hire purchase (HP) and leasing, apart from the nomenclature, are in the calculations and presentation. Whereas an HP contract is usually quoted with a simple interest rate, leasing is normally quoted with its true (amortised) compound rate.

Usually lenders (the hire purchase or leasing companies) require a deposit or some sort of advance payments by the borrower, to "show willing", and as we shall see this front-end requirement substantially affects the overall calculations.

The Hewlett-Packard *Manuals* point out that leasing calculations "typically use advance payments", but this implies one up-front payment only: in practice this is usually considered inadequate, the lender normally preferring three such payments. Where there is an advanced fee, whether an initial deposit or a series of advance payments, the subsequent payments are always "in arrears".

With hire purchase, as indeed the name implies, the goods are hired and are in fact deemed to have been fully purchased only when all the payments have been completed. Leasing, however, is a different concept in that the goods are leased and at all times remain the property of the lessor, the lessee returning the plant at the end of the term of the lease. In this case the plant can be written off as "scrap" (salvage), re-leased or sold "at best". In the latter case the leasing company will require the lessee to cover the sale value, called for contract purposes the "residual". If the residual was, say, £1,000 and the effective sale realised that amount, or more, the lessee would not be required to make any payments over and above his periodic (monthly or quarterly) instalments; but if the leasing company forecast the future sale value incorrectly then the lessee will be required to make up the difference.

The *Manuals* refer to the residual as "the option to purchase at the end of the leasing period", and if the lessee wishes to do so he can purchase the plant for the assumed residual value (on which the periodic payments were in part based) but, in the UK, it is unlikely that this action would appeal; for if the plant was purchased by the lessee at the end of the contract there would be no tax advantages.

I propose to delve no further into the UK tax system as it relates to hiring and leasing (if indeed such a conglomeration of rates, concessions and liabilities can be called a system). Suffice it to say that providing, and only providing, such arrangements are kept at arms' length some useful tax concessions can be obtained. If tax concessions are sought it is illegal for the lessee to bid, or to instruct an agent to bid, at public auction for plant or vehicles recently leased.

As most leasing contracts are between companies it is not normally necessary to provide the APR; but as most HP borrowing is by individuals, it will usually be a legal requirement to state the APR which must be carefully calculated; for the advertisements and the final agreed quotations are usually given as a "simple interest quote".

Hire purchase calculations

The general mechanisms of hire purchase agreements are relatively simple and are probably well known to those using this often expensive method of acquiring capital goods. But there are one or two minor anomalies, such as balloon payments and front-end fees which may complicate matters in some cases.

Key in the following **HP/LOANS * *** program:

```
H.P.LOANS:IF(S(COST) OR S(PMTS):(COST-DEP
)x(1+(FLAT%÷100xSGN(P)x#PER÷P))÷#PER-PMTS
:(COST-DEP)÷PMTS-(USPV(((((EFF÷100)+1)^I
NV(P))-1)x100xP)÷P:#PER)))
```

(Ensure a space before/after OR above)

| COST | DEP | FLAT% | P | #PER | MORE |
| PMTS | EFF | | | | MORE |

[#Per] is the total number of payments over the full term of loan. [P] is the number of payments made each year. If no deposit is required input zero to [DEP%].

Example: A high street purchase of, say, kitchen units for £764.71 with a 15% deposit and an HP contract over 24 months. If the quoted rate was 15% what are the monthly payments, the APR and TAP? Apart from finding the [PMTS], for which it was designed, the program provides the deposit amount (required for the TAP) and the cost less deposit (required for the APR).

SOLVE ↓↑ HP/LOANS CALC

Input the following values:
764.71 [x] 15 [%] [=] 114.706500: key-in 114.71 [INPUT] DEP

COST	DEP	FLAT%	P	#PER	MORE
764.71	114.71	15	12	24	

PMTS	EFF				MORE
?					

= 35.208333
Round Pmts 35.21 press PMTS then press EFF

EFF = 30.073808
APR = 30.0%

To find the TAP:

[RCL] PMTS x [RCL] #PER [+]
[RCL] DEP   [=] 959.75 TAP

Front-end fees
Front-end fees, being an extra charge, will affect the yield, and thus the APR. Repeat the calculation above on the in-built [TVM] program to find the interest rate but subtract the fees from the [PV]. Assume in this instance that the front-end fees are £65.

Assuming all values remain *in situ* from the last example

```
[RCL]  COST  [-] 65  COST  DON'T alter payments:
```

COST	DEP	FLAT%	P	#PER	MORE
699.71	114.71	15	12	24	

PMTS	EFF				MORE
35.21	? = 45.568112	APR = 45.5%			

I said earlier that HP could come expensive!

Occasionally the fees are covered by making them part of the payments. In this instance the new payments would become £35.21 + 65/24 = £37.92; and the effective rate would be calculated as 40.729787% effective = 40.7 APR.

Any small registration fee required for high street HP is almost always paid together with the deposit: subtract such fees from the loan when recalculating the APR. In the case of more expensive lending, with an insurance element contract, front-end fees are usually paid with the first payment (see below).

Hire purchase balloon payments

If an end payment is required – a balloon payment over and above the normal monthly instalments – the quotation should be, and usually is, at the true rate and the periodic payments can calculated by the conventional [TVM] annuities ordinary amortisation formula. However, should the quote be given (abnormally) as a flat rate, the flat rate must be converted to a true rate before considering the balloon factor – and the program, FLAT/NOM/EFF outlined in Chapter 1 may be found useful. (The section "A simple interest quotation" in the leasing section, later in this chapter, also refers.)

Assume a £1,000 HP loan over a period of 24 months at a 20% true nominal rate (APR 21.9%) with a balloon payment of £100. Using the [TVM] discipline the payments are:

[EXIT]	FIN	TVM	OTHER	1	P/YR	END	[EXIT]
N	I%YR	PV	PMT		FV	OTHER	
24	20/12	-1000	?		100		
			= 47.47				

When HP is related to the more expensive purchases, such as private cars, etc, as opposed to the conventional high street HP, the balloon payments are sometimes paid not at the end of the term but one period later. The likely reason for the delayed payment is fully outlined in the section on "The final payment option" under "Leasing" below. In that case the equation is the same as the above, save that the discounting of the balloon is for one period longer – perhaps for 25 months instead of 24 for example.

N	I%YR	PV	PMT	FV	OTHER
25	20/12	?	0	−100	

$$= 66.15$$
$$66.15 - 1,000 = -933.85 \text{ PV}$$

N	I%YR	PV	PMT	FV	OTHER
24	20/12	−933.85	?	0	

$$= 47.53 \text{ pmts with a delayed option}$$

Insurance premiums

For the more expensive types of HP it may be thought convenient to insure against the purchaser being unable to meet his monthly payments, owing to sickness or temporary unemployment. In that case a finance house, through the hire purchase company, will arrange a small additional premium, with a consequent slight increase in monthly payments. The amount of the premium is usually related to the term of the loan, the rate being, say, 6% for one year, or 8.50% for 3 years.

Example: Assume that a car is purchased for £6,250.00, that there is no part exchange required but there is an agreed 20% deposit, making a total required repayment of £6,250 – (6,250 x .20) = 6,250 – 1,250 = £5000.00. The quoted simple interest rate is 12% over the three years and so the payments are 5000 x (1 + (12/100 x 3))= £6,800 and this amount, divided by 36 months, equals monthly payments of £188.89 (188.888888).

Without any insurance premium the true rate (and APR) and the total charge for credit are found as follows:

```
▌ [EXIT] ↓↑ H.P.LOANS  CALC
6250 [x] 20 [%] [=]  1,250  press   DEP
 COST   DEP   FLAT%    P    #PER    MORE
 6250  1,250    12    12     36
 PMTS   EFF                         MORE
   ?
   = 188.89
```

To find the "real cost" for calculation purposes:

```
 COST   DEP   FLAT%   #PER    P    PMTS
   ?      0       (leave values unaltered)
   = 5,000.00
```

and to find the APR:

```
 COST   DEP   FLAT%    P    #PER   MORE
 5000     0     12    12     36
 PMTS   EFF                        MORE
188.89    ?  = 23.386595   APR = 23.3%
£(188.89 x 36) + 1,250     TAP = £8,050.04
```

In the event that insurance was required, at an agreed rate of 8.50% over a three year term, the premium would be £653.55 and the new payments £213.58 – determined by:

$$188.89 \times 36 \times .085 \quad = 578.00 \text{ (factor)}$$

$$578.00 \times \frac{5,000}{5,000 - 578} \quad = 653.55 \quad \text{premium}$$

$$578.00 \times 1.130710 \quad = 653.55 \quad \text{premium}$$
$$188.89 \times 1.130710 \quad = 213.58 \quad \text{new pmts}$$

Key in the following **HP/INSUR** program:

```
H.P.INSUR:PMTSx(COST-DEP)÷((COST-DEP)-(PMT
Sx#PERxINS%÷100))=N/P
```

```
     PMTS  COST   DEP   #PER   INS%   N/P
```

```
   [N/P] = NEW payments, with a insurance content.
      (All values are shared with HP/LOANS)
```

Taking the above example:

PMTS	COST	DEP	#PER	INS%	N/P
188.89	6250	1250	36	**8.5**	?
(RND)					= 213.58 (213.579992)

To find the "premium" revert to the HP/LOANS program:

[EXIT]	↓↑ HP/LOANS	CALC	Round	pmts [INPUT]	
COST	DEP%	FLAT%	P	#PER	MORE
?	0	12	12	36	
= 5,653.59					

PMTS	EFF				MORE
213.58	and	5,653.59 − 5,000 = £653.59			

As the above is a *pro rata* calculation the APR will be the same as before, namely 23.3%. If a front-end fee is required this must be subtracted from the capital amount and the equation re-calculated as above, provided, and only provided, that this fee is paid at the outset. Unfortunately the practice, with this type of contract, is that such fees are normally paid with the first payment – which, being an HP contract, is always paid in arrears.

Consequently the only correct method of establishing the monthly rate, and hence the APR, is to calculate by a discounted cash flow discipline, [CFLO]. The good news is, however, that the difference in the internal rate of return between treating the payment as if paid at the outset, or paid with the first payment, is normally so small as not to affect the APR. Nevertheless, if in doubt, the correct method is to employ a DCF calculation.

Leasing calculations

The rate of interest for leasing contracts is usually quoted at the true nominal rate, seldom as simple interest – but see the "simple interest quote" section below.

Only if a leasing contract is made to an individual member of the public, rather than to a company, is it necessary to provide the APR and TAP. If so, it is a simple matter to convert the quoted nominal rate to the effective (and hence, truncating to one place of decimals, to find the APR).

In hire purchase agreements there is usually a reasonably substantial deposit required, indeed sometimes a front-end fee as well. The repayments, in consequence, are always in arrears. With leasing, however, the conventional calculation is for payments in advance, namely one advance payment only. Since most lessors consider that a single payment in advance is a somewhat meagre form of deposit they prefer a larger initial payment. There is no conventional way of deciding the size of this initial payment but the most fashionable arrangement appears to be "three payments in advance".

But having decided on, say, three advance payments, because the norm for leasing contracts is one advance payment, it is clear that there are two, as opposed to three, extra advance payments. As there will be the same number of payment periods, irrespective of advance payments, there will be two, as opposed to three, non payment periods. The question is when are these non payment periods to occur in the life of the loan, at the beginning of the lease, *initial* pause, as it is called; – at the end of the lease, *terminal* pause; or are the payments to be *spread* over the whole term? Below are the various methods of calculation with examples.

Once there are a number of advance payments, in place of the the one conventional payment in advance, all subsequent payments will be in arrears – for it would be absurd to demand a number of advance payments and then expect yet one more payment in advance merely because of the conventional method of calculating leasings!

"In lieu" options

Some traders sometimes prefer to make a substantial initial down payment in lieu of a number of advanced payments; but because they have become accustomed to the benefits arising from one or other of the above options they require the same method of non period payments. So not only has the leasing company to calculate the payments required in respect of a substantial down payment but also the type of payment required, initial or terminal pause, or the overall spread.

The final payment option – the label [EXTRA]

Unhappily, there is still yet one further option! First, a short scenario of what might happen in practice, sometimes a little different from what happens in theory!

Suppose, for example, that the leasing arrangements were related to motor vehicles which the local garage would sell to an individual purchaser. If terms were required the garage would in all probability take out an HP loan from a finance company and then pass on that cost to the purchaser by means of a leasing contract. The purchaser is thus no longer a purchaser but is now the lessee. So far so good.

In the general remarks at the beginning of this chapter readers will recall that if the leased item did not realise its full residual value on disposal the lessee might be required to make up the difference. The point is, when will the garage know whether or not they will need to ask a lessee to make up the amount, – i.e. when will they know whether the vehicle has achieved the stated residual value on resale?

The garage, receiving back the car at the end of the term, is likely to take a month to clean it up and take it to auction – and not until then will they know whether to ask the lessee for payment. Thus they could be "out of the money" for a period. "Charges" at this stage, on top of everything else, could be counter productive! So what can be done?

The conventional way out of this dilemma, and this really is the last remaining option (!), is to assume that the vehicle is returned one month later.

For example, at the end of the 36th month the residual will be calculated as if it is not due until the end of the 37th month. This will, of course, increase the payments to an extent considered sufficient to cover the lessor being out of the money by one month.

In the terminal pause example below, instead of re-calculating the whole structure of the loan to ensure the "extra" residual month, the same payments would be due if the residual was reduced by £13.56. Alternatively, if the residual was reduced by £50 the payments would rise by only £1.

One might wonder why any distributor should bother about the extra month's calculation in order to uplift the overall term payments by such a small sum. The difference, in the example under reference, being only 28 pence per month, or just over £10 for 36 months on a £10,000 contract. If a large distributor, however, moved 250 vehicles a month, every year, £10 a month x 250 x 12 months = £30,000 a year!

Advance payments with all the various options
If we take one simple example throughout, in respect of all the various options, hopefully, confusion will avoided.

Example: A leasing contract for £10,000 (assuming no deposits) with a £1,000 residual, commencing April 15 over a term of 36 months, at a true rate of 16.50%. Three advance payments are required. (If a down payment is required in lieu of advance payments assume the front-end amount is £3,000.)

Key in the following **LEASING** program:

```
LEASING:((CAP-LIEU)-RESxSPPV(RATE%÷P:(#PE
R+IF(EXTRA=1:1:0))))÷IF(TYPE<>3:((USPV(RA
TE%÷P:#PER-#ADV))xIF(TYPE=1:((1+RATE%÷100
÷P))^-(#ADV-1):1))+IF(LIEU<>0:0:#ADV):((U
SPV(RATE%÷P:#PER))x(1+RATE%÷100÷P)+(#ADV-
1)))=PMTS
```

CAP	LIEU	RES	RATE%	P	MORE
#PER	EXTRA	TYPE	#ADV	PMTS	MORE

The conventional method TYPE 0 (*one* payment in advance)
This assumes that there is one payment in advance to be paid
on April 15. The 35 following payments will be then made
commencing a month later on May 15, and on the 15th day of
the 36th month the plant will be returned to the lessor –
together with any residual payment applicable.

CAP	LIEU	RES	RATE%	P	MORE
10000	0	1000	16.50	12	
#PER	EXTRA	TYPE	#ADV	PMTS	MORE
36	0	0	1	?	

= 327.88 (BEGIN)

For payments in arrears input 0 to [#ADV] – occasionally
required (see in lieu payments below).

The above payments could, of course, also be found on the
Hewlett-Packard [TVM] discipline:

[EXIT] [EXIT] FIN TVM OTHER 12 P/YR press BEG
      [EXIT] N I%YR PV PMT FV OTHER
         36 16.5 –10000 ? 1000

= 327.88 (BEGIN)

OTHER press END
      [EXIT] N I%YR PV PMT FV OTHER
         36 16.5 –10000 ? 1000

= 332.39 (END)

and reverting to the LEASING program:

[EXIT] SOLVE ↓↑ LEASING CALC

CAP	LIEU	RES	RATE%	P	MORE
10000	0	1000	16.50	12	
#PER	EXTRA	TYPE	#ADV	PMTS	MORE
36	0	0	0	?	

= 332.39 (END)

The initial pause TYPE 1 (all subsequent payments in arrears)
This assumes that there are three payments in advance, made on April 15. No payments will be made for the next two months and the subsequent 33 payments will commence on July 15. At the end of the 36th month the plant will be returned to the lessor – together with any residual payment applicable.

CAP	LIEU	RES	RATE%	P	MORE
10000	0	1000	16.50	12	press
#PER	EXTRA	TYPE	#ADV	PMTS	MORE
36	0	1	3	?	

= 327.42 (initial)

The residual's "extra" month

CAP	LIEU	RES	RATE%	P	MORE
10000	0	1000	16.50	12	press
#PER	EXTRA	TYPE	#ADV	PMTS	MORE
36	**1**	1	3	?	

= 327.71 (initial)

For £3,000 front-end deposit in lieu of advance payments

CAP	LIEU	RES	RATE%	P	MORE
10000	**3000**	1000	16.50	12	
#PER	EXTRA	TYPE	#ADV	PMTS	MORE
36	0	1	3	?	

= 248.83 (initial)

CAP	LIEU	RES	RATE%	P	MORE
10000	3000	1000	16.50	12	press
#PER	EXTRA	TYPE	#ADV	PMTS	MORE
36	**1**	1	3	?	

= 249.15 (initial)

The terminal pause TYPE 2 (all subsequent payments in arrears)
This method is the converse of the initial pause above, in that
the non payment periods are at the end of the term. In this
case the three advance payments are made on April 15 and
the further 33 payments commence on May 15. No payments
are made at the end of the 34th and 35th months and the
plant is returned to the lessor at the end of the 36th month,
together with any residual amount if applicable. (Of the three
different methods for non payment periods this option
appears to be the most popular.)

CAP	LIEU	RES	RATE%	P	MORE
10000	0	1000	16.50	12	
#PER	EXTRA	TYPE	#ADV	PMTS	MORE
36	0	2	3	?	

= 319.50 (terminal)

The residual's "extra" month

CAP	LIEU	RES	RATE%	P	MORE
10000	0	1000	16.50	12	press
#PER	EXTRA	TYPE	#ADV	PMTS	MORE
36	**1**	2	3	?	

= 319.78 (terminal)

For £3,000 front-end deposit in lieu of advance payments

CAP	LIEU	RES	RATE%	P	MORE
10000	**3000**	1000	16.50	12	
#PER	EXTRA	TYPE	#ADV	PMTS	MORE
36	0	2	3	?	

= 242.12 (terminal)

CAP	LIEU	RES	RATE%	P	MORE
10000	3000	1000	16.50	12	press
#PER	EXTRA	TYPE	#ADV	PMTS	MORE
36	**1**	2	3	?	

= 242.44 (terminal)

The spread method TYPE 3 (all subsequent payments in arrears)
This assumes that there are three payments in advance, made
on April 15. The remaining 35 payments, spread evenly over
the full term, will commence on May 15: at the end of the 36th
month the plant will be returned to the lessor, together with
any residual amount applicable.

CAP	LIEU	RES	RATE%	P	MORE
10000	0	1000	16.50	12	
#PER	EXTRA	TYPE	#ADV	PMTS	MORE
36	0	3	3	?	

= 306.47 (spread)

The residual's extra month

CAP	LIEU	RES	RATE%	P	MORE
10000	0	1000	16.50	12	press
#PER	EXTRA	TYPE	#ADV	PMTS	MORE
36	**1**	3	3	?	

= 306.75 (spread)

With up-front in lieu payments, it would obviously be absurd
to expect yet further front-end payments; therefore with in
lieu payments all subsequent payments are in arrears. And
the spread requirements become an annuities ordinary, [END],
calculation, a conventional straight loan of £7,000 over 36
months, with a balloon payment of £1,000 – which of course
can be checked on the [TVM] discipline

For £3,000 front end deposit in lieu of advance payments

CAP	LIEU	RES	RATE%	P	MORE
10000	**3000**	1000	16.50	12	
#PER	EXTRA	TYPE	#ADV	PMTS	MORE
36	0	**0**	**0**	?	

= 226.18 (spread)

CAP	LIEU	RES	RATE%	P	MORE
10000	3000	1000	16.50	12	press
#PER	EXTRA	TYPE	#ADV	PMTS	MORE
36	**1**	**0**	**0**	?	

= 226.47 (spread)

A number of up-front payments different to the number of non-payments required

If a lessee wished to make 3 advance payments but to have, say, 5 pauses before the first payment how can the correct initial payments be found on the LEASING program?

CAP	LIEU	RES	RATE%	P	MORE
10000	0	1000	16.5	12	

#PER	EXTRA	TYPE	#ADV	PMTS	MORE
36	0	1	3	?	

= 327.42 x 3 = 982.25 press LIEU

CAP	LIEU	RES	RATE%	P	MORE
10000	928.25	1000	16.5	12	

#PER	EXTRA	TYPE	#ADV	PMTS	MORE
36	0	1	**5**	?	

= 353.68 thereafter

Because the front-end payments no longer balance the non-payment periods, the subsequent payments will need some final adjustments.

One option is to adjust the advance payments to £350 or £355, which will consequently require in lieu payments of:

CAP	LIEU	RES	RATE%	P	MORE
10000	?	1000	16.5	12	

#PER	EXTRA	TYPE	#ADV	PMTS	MORE
36	0	1	5	350	LIEU = 1,069.83
				355	= 951.00

Unhappily, if spread payments are required the calculation cannot be the same as that for initial or terminal pauses.

First find the value of the spread payments as was done for the initial pause calculation above:

CAP	LIEU	RES	RATE%	P	MORE
10000	0	1000	16.5	12	

#PER	EXTRA	TYPE	#ADV	PMTS	MORE
36	0	3	3	?	

306.47 (rounded)

The 3 advance payments represent 306.47 x 3 = 919.41 the in lieu value.

But, earlier, it was shown that any spread calculation with in lieu payments becomes a conventional annuities ordinary, [END], loan and that consequently (0) is input to both the [TYPE] and [#ADV] labels.

With 0 in [#ADV] how can a loan, with 5 non-payment periods at the beginning of the contract, posssibly be calculated by the program? The simple answer is that it cannot!

The only method is to employ the [TVM] program. In that case the loan, less the in lieu payments, becomes the Present Value. In this example, with a [PV] of £9,080.59, and with no payments over the next five months, the new balance becomes:

▌[EXIT]	FIN	TVM	OTHER	12	P/YR	END	[EXIT]
N	I%YR	PV	PMT	FV			
5	16.5	−9080.59	0	?			
				= 9,722.29			

After rearranging the equation we get:

N	I%YR	PV	PMT	FV
31	16.5	−9722.27	?	1000
			= 361.23 payments required.	

A discounted cash flow result will validate the above calculation:

```
[EXIT] [EXIT]  FIN    CFLO  ▌ [CLEAR DATA] "CLEAR THE LIST?"  YES
919.41 − 10,000 = −9,080.59 [INPUT]
0 INPUT] 5 [INPUT]   361.23   [INPUT] 30 [INPUT]
1,000 + 361.23 = 1,335.66   [INPUT]      [INPUT]
[EXIT]  CALC   IRR%  = 1.375022 x 12 = 16.500266%
```

The minor decimal discrepancy is due to rounding of the payments.

If values require to be adusted the statistician can work backwards through the equations above.

Finding the balances
Current balances can be found on the [TVM], [CFLO], and [AMRT] in-built programs. A special "balance" program can, however, be supplied if required.

Employing the same basic example used in all the above calculations, find the balances at the end of the 24th month.

The conventional method (with one payment in advance)
The payment is £327.88 monthly.

First find the balance by [AMRT] – then by [CFLO]:

```
 N    I%YR   PV    PMT      FV  OTHER 12 P/YR   BEG  [EXIT] <--
 24   16.50  10000 -327.88  1000
OTHER AMRT  24  #P   BAL   = 4,441.74
```

Alternatively, by discounted cash flow methods:

```
█ [MAIN]  FIN  CFLO █ [CLEAR DATA]  YES
FLOW(0) will equal 327.88 -10000 = -9,672.12
FLOW(1)   "     "    327.88
TIMES(1)  "     "     23.00
With 16.5/12 input to   I%  the  NFV  will show as = -4,441.74
```

But probably the simplest and quickest method is to use the [TVM] discipline, Remember the conventional method is one payment in advance [BEGIN] and therefore the [FV] must be divided by $(1 + i/p)$ which in this case gives $1 + (16.50/1200)$ = 1.013750

```
█ [MAIN]  FIN  TVM
```

Providing [TVM] has not been used since the previous calculation the values remain as previously input.

```
 N    I%YR   PV    PMT      FV   OTHER
 24   16.50  10000 -327.88  ?
                            = 4,502.81

and 4,502.81/1.013750       = 4,441.74
                             BAL (24)
```

The initial pause (with three payments in advance)
The monthly payments are 327.42 [STO 8] and the [PV] is
therefore (327.42 x 3) – 10,000 = –9,017.74 [STO 7]. There
were two pause months before payments start, consequently
with zero payments there are two periods of interest only –
with no off-set payments. Therefore the correct [PV] at the
actual start of payments:

N	I%YR	PV	PMT	FV	OTHER
					press

press 12 P/YR **END** [EXIT] <--

N	I%YR	PV	PMT	FV	OTHER
2	(16.50)	[RCL7]	0	?	
		–9,017.74		= 9,267.43	

[+/−] press PV [RCL8] press PMT

N	I%YR	PV	PMT	FV	OTHER
22	16.50	**–9267.43**	327.42	?	
				= 4,170.13	

Employing the [CFLO] program the cash flows are:

```
FLOW(0) will equal –9,017.74
FLOW(1)   "     "      0.00
TIMES(1)  "     "      2.00
FLOW(2)   "     "    327.42
TIMES(2)  "     "     22.00
```

and with 16.5/12 input to I% the NFV will show as = 4,170.13
BAL (24)

The terminal pause (with three payments in advance)
Subtract the three advance payments from the capital sum and then employ either the [TVM] program, the amortised schedule [AMRT] or the [CFLO] program. They will naturally all give the same answer! The monthly payments are £319.50, consequently the [PV] will be: (319.50 x 3) – 10,000 = –9,041.50
Key-in the data:

N	I%YR	PV	PMT	FV	OTHER
24	16.50	–9041.5	319.50	?	
		[STO7]	[STO8]	= 3,536.10	

and press OTHER AMRT 24 #P BAL
= 3,536.10

or ▮ [MAIN] FIN CFLO ▮ [CLEAR DATA]
[RCL7] [INPUT] [RCL8] [INPUT] 24 [INPUT]
[EXIT] CALC
and with 16.5/12 input to I% the NFV will show as = 3,536.10
BAL (24)

The spread method (with three payments in advance)
In this case the payments are £306.47 monthly and so with three payments in advance the capital sum, [PV] is 306.47 [STO 8] and (306.47 x 3) – 10,000 = –9,080.59 [STO 7] (Providing [TVM] has not been used since the previous calc: values remain.)

N	I%YR	PV	PMT	FV	OTHER
(24)	(16.50)	[RCL7]	[RCL8]	?	
		–9080.59	306.47	= 3,957.89	
			BAL (24)		

Balances for the extra residual month
Balances with the "extra" residual month pose no problem; for the slightly higher payments already take into account any difference in calculation. The terminal balance above of £3,536.10 becomes a balance of £3,528.20 from payments of £319.78

An example from the Hewlett-Packard Manuals

All the calculations above have, for simplicity's sake, been related to one example only. On page 93, HP-19B *Manual* and page 65 HP-17B *Manual* a leasing example is given which is calculated in four steps using the [TVM] discipline. Having the leasing program available the answer can naturally be provided somewhat more quickly.   A company leases a machine for 4 years. The monthly payments are $2,400 with two payments in advance with a residual of $15,000 at the end of the leasing period (treat as terminal, type 2). The question is what is the capitalised value of the lease?   The rate for borrowing is 18% nominal.

[MAIN]	SOLVE	↓↑	LEASING	CALC	
CAP	LIEU	RES	RATE%	P	MORE
?	0	15000	18	12	
= 91,476.00					
#PER	EXTRA	TYPE	#ADV	PMTS	MORE
12x4	0	2	2	2400	

A simple interest quote

Usually leasing quotations are at the true rate of interest, as indeed are all the examples above.   But recently, with high rates of borrowing, some leasing companies think it makes commercial sense to quote their rates at simple interest, especially as hire purchase rates are so quoted and in the motor vehicle industry HP and leasing are inextricably intermixed.

What difference does this make?   Very little, save that the simple interest rates look somewhat more attractive – to the uninitiated!

Before any calculations are made to find the payments derived from any of the options outlined above, the simple interest rate must be converted to a true nominal rate. This is done by finding the simple interest payments and then finding the true rate thereof.

For example, a simple interest quote of 15% over a term of 3 years with monthly payments will find a true rate of nearly 26%, certainly a substantial rate of return to the lessor.

How is that rate determined? The simple interest payments can best be determined based on £100, not necessarily the loan amount of the contract lease.

$$\frac{100 + (100 \times .15 \times 3)}{3 \times 12} = 4.027778 \text{ pmts}$$

[MAIN]	FIN	TVM	12 P/YR	END MODE	on display
N	I%YR	PV	PMT	FV	OTHER
36	?	−100	4.02778	0	
	= 25.975889				

But the simplest method is to use the FLAT/NOM/EFF program outlined in Chapter 1 and repeated below to save referring back.

```
FLAT/NOM/EFF:IF(S(FLAT%) OR S(TRUE%):((IN
V(FLAT%xYEARS÷100+1))xSGN(TRUE%)xYEARSxP)
—USPV(TRUE%÷P:YEARSxP):((SPFV(NOM%÷P:P)—1
)x100)—EFF%)
```

(Ensure a space before/after OR above)
(The [P] factor is common to both parts of the program)

FLAT%	YEARS	TRUE%	P		NOM%	EFF%
15	3	?	12			
	= 25.975889 [input]					
				press		
				?		
				= 29.302880		

With the true nominal rate the calculations to find the payments, with all the options available, can now commence. The lessor really has two options, one is to ask a simple interest rate a little less than the true "going rate" and collect a substantial return. This method will not be overlooked for long and is unlikely to be popular with clients!

The alternative option, and indeed normal practice, is to determine the "true" return required and work backwards to find the equivalent simple interest rate.

Assume that the going borrowing rate was around 16.50% and, with quarterly payments over a term of 5 years, is in the general neighbourhood of the return a lessor requires. In that case he could quote a flat rate of:

FLAT%	YEARS	TRUE%	P	NOM%	EFF%
?	5	16.50	4	16.50	?
= 9.759401					= 17.549303

On checking the effective return the lessor decided that he could wear an effective return of 17.5% so:

FLAT%	YEARS	TRUE%	P	NOM%	EFF%
			4	?	17.50
				= 16.456321	

Checking the flat rate, if the true rate was precisely 16.45%:

FLAT%	YEARS	TRUE%	P	NOM%	EFF%
?	5	16.45	4		
= 9.726648					

and, if it is decided that an exact simple interest rate of 9.73% would be suitable, what is the APR?

FLAT%	YEARS	TRUE%	P	NOM%	EFF%
9.73	5	?	4		
		= 16.455119			
		[INPUT] press	?	= 17.498643 APR = 17.4%	

Making a factor list
A salesman, in a large firm of distributors, discussing with a client the various options available for a leasing contract will probably have a PC on his desk to undertake the calculations outlined above. Other firms may provide their salesmen with programmable calculators, such as the HP-17 or 19B, or bespoke calculators, with specific leasing modules, especially if such salesmen were not necessarily desk-bound.

Some of the smaller firms, however, compete quite nicely with "factors". Instead of using a computer or calculator the salesman simply employs his factors list.

What exactly are these factors? A computer, or HP calculator, is initially used to fabricate them, but once they are listed all that is necessary is find the relevant ones.

The basic value is taken as £1,000 and payments for a leasing contract are calculated at various rates, employing the various options outlined above. Assume that a 16½% rate over 36 months, with three advance payments, terminal type, was required. Employing the leasing program above the payments will be found as 34.0311356137. Dividing these payments by the capital value, the factor becomes 0.034031 [STO 1].

CAP	LIEU	RES	RATE%	P	MORE
1000	0	0	16.5	12	
#PER	EXTRA	TYPE	#ADV	PMTS	MORE
36	0	2	3	?	PMTS = 34.03

Do the same calculation with a £1,000 residual *but with no capital value* and payments will be found as 20.8144635243. Divide by 1,000 to find 0.020814 as the next factor [STO 2].

CAP	LIEU	RES	RATE%	P	MORE
0	0	−1000			
#PER	EXTRA	TYPE	#ADV	PMTS	MORE
	0			?	PMTS = 20.81

Now assume that a salesmen is discussing with a client the cost of a £25,000 leasing contract with a £2,500 residual; having the same parameters as above, namely 16.50%, three (terminal) payments in advance, over 36 months. Using the above factors in order to find the payments all he does is:

$$[RCL\ 1] \times 25,000 - [RCL\ 2] \times 2,500 = £798.74$$

And checking on the leasing program:

CAP	LIEU	RES	RATE%	P	MORE
25000	0	2500	16.50	12	
#PER	EXTRA	TYPE	#ADV	PMTS	MORE
36	0	2	3	?	
					PMTS = 798.74

Listing factors can, therefore, be made by the above methods, for any or all of the options outlined earlier in the chapter. The factors should correctly, for payment accuracy, be calculated to not less than 6 decimal places; but the industry usually reduces to 5 places, adding one penny to the resulting payments. For contracts over £100,000 the payments are generally rounded up/down to pounds only, the pence being ignored.

The statistician, using the HP-17B, may find it convenient to use the rounding program, outlined in the Introduction.

A leasing scenario
A leasing company was telephoned one morning by an old and valued client requesting a quotation for the lease of a £10,000 bulldozer over a period of the next five years.

The finance director figured that the commercial value of the type of dozer mentioned would be, at the end of five years, £1,000 and so treated this as the residual. The current arrangements for the leasing company were quarterly payments at a nominal rate of 15%. But as the client was well known to the firm it was decided not to charge any up-front payments but to arrange a conventional contract (annuities due [BEGIN] – one payment only in advance). Reaching for his HP-17B the finance director worked out the payments required:

[MAIN]	SOLVE	↓↑	LEASING	CALC	
CAP	LIEU	RES	RATE%	P	MORE
10000	0	1000	15	4	
#PER	EXTRA	TYPE	#ADV	PMTS	MORE
20	0	0	1	?	PMTS=660.39

On telephoning to his opposite number in the client firm with this payment quotation, he met some disappointment; for it appeared that his clients had also done some figuring as what they reckoned the payments should be – and this was £600 per quarter for the 5 years.

The finance director, privately wondering whether it was a try-on and he was being taken for a ride, or if they had received a quotation elsewhere, replied he'd "see what he could do and come back to them."

Back to the 17B. What percentage return would £600 give his firm?

CAP	LIEU	RES	RATE%	P	MORE	
10000	0	1000	?	4		RATE%=10.86

#PER	EXTRA	TYPE	#ADV	PMTS	MORE
20	0	0	1	600	

The board would never wear that return: . . . . timing?

CAP	LIEU	RES	RATE%	P	MORE
10000	0	1000	15	4	

#PER	EXTRA	TYPE	#ADV	PMTS	MORE	
?	0	0	1	600		#PER=23.37

Telephoning his client again he was told somewhat acidly that if they'd wanted a term of nearly six years they've have asked for it in the first place.

What about messing about with the residual; after all £1,000 was only an intelligent guess in the first instance:

CAP	LIEU	RES	RATE%	P	MORE	
10000	0	?	15	4		RATE%=2,818.20

#PER	EXTRA	TYPE	#ADV	PMTS	MORE
20	0	0	1	600	

Intelligent or not, thought the director, no one in his right mind could imagine that the dozer could sell for £2,800 after 5 years – not the way they treat their equipment.

The only other possibility would seem to be "advance payments": 4 payments?

CAP	LIEU	RES	RATE%	P	MORE
10000	0	1000	15	4	

#PER	EXTRA	TYPE	#ADV	PMTS	MORE	
20	0	2	4	?		PMTS=599.94

Just as the finance director, not very hopefully, was about to ask his client if they'd wear an up-front payment of around of £2,400 one of his staff brought in a message from the dozer makers to say they had a six-month-old dozer of the type required, a bit scratched but otherwise as new, for £9,000. "And are you interested?"

The return? "Don't forget to adjust the residual", murmured the director to himself, 10% presumably?

CAP	LIEU	RES	RATE%	P	MORE	
9000	0	900	?	4		RATE%=15.42
#PER	EXTRA	TYPE	#ADV	PMTS	MORE	
20	0	0	1	600		

Retaining the 15% required return what are the payments?

CAP	LIEU	RES	RATE%	P	MORE	
9000	0	900	15	4		
#PER	EXTRA	TYPE	#ADV	PMTS	MORE	
20	0	0	1	?		PMTS=594.35

"Well", thought the director, "for their required £600 a quarter I'll ask if they'll accept the used dozer as suggested, and only if they are sticky will I mention the lower payments of £594.35."

Value Added Tax of 15%

In some circumstances VAT will be due on the payments. Individual companies will be well aware if/when this applies to them. With (gross) payments on display key in:

$$[+]\ 15\ [\%]\ [=]\ PMTS + VAT.$$

Should the user wish to have key-in facilities, add the following steps to the end of the LEASING program:

```
For   =PMTS   read   =PMTS÷(1+VAT÷100)
```

To find the value of PMTS + VAT input 15 to the additional label [VAT]. Otherwise this register should hold 0.

Skipped payment calculations

When considering whether to lease or not some companies realise that the plant they propose to hire cannot be used for parts of the year and that, irrespective of the resulting lack of cash flow, the monthly payments must be met on time.

For example, if a bulldozer was hired in October it might well be that the weather would prevent it being used during the three months commencing January. In that case the lessor might well agree that the payments for the months when the plant was out of action could be "skipped". How are the new payments, naturally somewhat greater than the normal payments spread over the whole year, to be determined?

Key in the following **SKIP * *** program:

```
SKIP:IF(S(CAP) OR S(DUE):(((CAP—(RESxSPPV
(RATE%÷P:#PER)))x(SPFV(RATE%÷P:P)—1)))÷((
USFV(RATE%÷P:BEFORE)xSPFV(RATE%÷P:(P—BEFO
RE))+USFV(RATE%÷P:AFTER))x(1—SPPV(RATE%÷P
:#PER)))÷(1+RATE%÷P÷100)—DUE:DUEx(1+(RATE
%÷P÷100)—ORD)⟩
```

(Ensure a space before/after OR above)

CAP	RES	RATE%	P	#PER	MORE
BEFOR	AFTER	DUE	ORD		MORE

Users may find the program above, and the discipline below, simpler than that outlined in the HP *Real Estate Banking and Leasing Solutions Manual* (page 130).

Example: Assume a capital amount of £10,000 with a residual of £3,000 at a rate of 15% nominal with monthly payments over 5 years: the payments commence October and the months January – March (inclusive) are skipped.

October – December	(3 months)	
January – March	(3 months)	SKIPPED
April – September	(6 months)	

This means there are 3 months before the skipping starts and there are 6 payments after the skipping has finished.

[MAIN]	SOLVE	↓↑	SKIP	CALC	
CAP	RES	RATE%	P	#PER	MORE
10000	3000	15	12	5x12	
BEFOR	AFTER	DUE	ORD		
3	6	?	?	DUE = 270.30 ✓	
				ORD = 273.68 ✓	

To find the payments in arrears multiply by (1 + i/p), and in this example: £270.30 x 1.0125 = £273.68

With a skipped payment structured contract the payments are conventionally required to be in advance, namely one advance payment, [BEGIN], annuities due.

With such a structure a number of payments in advance are obviously impractical but it is not unknown that a front-end deposit is required in lieu; in that event all subsequent payments will be in arrears [END], annuities ordinary.

Taking the above example, but substituting quarterly payments over a term of two years:

CAP	RES	RATE%	P	#PER	MORE
10000	3000	15	4	2x4	
BEFOR	AFTER	DUE	ORD		
1	2	?			
		= 1,475.69			

If there is no residual input 0.00 to [RES], press [DUE] = 1,900.36

Notes

(1) The values in the SKIP program are shared with the LEASING program, so users can transfer from one to another as required.

(2) The payments cannot be rounded in the program, in case the capital value is required to be found from given payments; consequently manual rounding must be executed.

Formula

$$\frac{(loan - (res \times (1 + i/p)^{-np})) \times ((1 + i/p)^{p} - 1)}{(s_{\underline{}a|} \times (1 + i/p)^{(p-a)}) + s_{\underline{}b|}} \times \frac{1}{1-(1 + i/p)^{-np}}$$

$$= \text{pmts in arrears}$$

Where (a) = # of pmts *before* skipping commences

(b) = # of pmts *after* skipping concludes

(p) = # of compounding periods in any one year

(np) = # of periods in a *full term*

(res) = residual

$$s_{\underline{}np|} = \frac{(1 + i/p) - 1}{i/p} \quad \text{(savings ordinary)}$$

Taking the above monthly example:

$$\frac{(10,000-(3,000 \times 1.0125^{-60})) \times (1.0125^{12}-1)}{[((1.0125^{3}-1)/.0125) \times 1.0125^{9}]+[(1.0125^{6}-1)/.0125]} \times \frac{1}{1-1.0125^{-60}}$$

$$= \text{pmts in arrears}$$

$$\frac{1,378.68}{9.587642} \times \frac{1}{0.525432} = 273.67 \text{ (ORD)}$$

$$273.67/1.0125 = 270.30 \text{ (DUE)}$$

Factor lists, if required, can be made for skipped payments in the same way as factor lists were made for conventional leasing, see above.

A validity check

For verification, use a discounted cash flow calculation and work with an annual perspective, employing the effective rate.

If employing the HP [cflo] in-built discipline:

▌ [MAIN] FIN   CFLO ▌ [CLEAR DATA]   CLEAR THE LIST? YES

```
FLOW(0)=?    0    [INPUT]
FLOW(1)=?    1    [INPUT]
#TIMES(1)=? 3    [INPUT]
FLOW(2)=?    0    [INPUT]
#TIMES(2)=? 3    [INPUT]
FLOW(3)=?    1    [INPUT]
#TIMES(3)=? 6    [INPUT]
```

```
[EXIT]  CALC
15 [÷] 12                I%
press                    NFV   = 9.587642 [STO] 0
```

[EXIT]   [EXIT]   TVM   OTHER   1 P/YR press   END   [EXIT]
<---   9.587642 on display [+/–]   PMT   (or [RCL 0] [+/–] PMT)

N	I/YR	PV	PMT	FV	OTHER
5	16.07452	?	–9.59	0	
		= 31.337581			

    16.07452, being the effective of 15% nominal

and with £10,000 less the discounted residual of £3,000 equalling £8,576.30:

    £8,576.30 ÷ 31.337581 = £273.67 ord
                ÷ 1.0125000 = £270.30 due   Q.E.D.

The actuarial methods employed above for calculating hire purchase, HP insurance and leasing contracts are used now by General Motors Acceptance Corporation (UK) Ltd. The examples above, however, are in no way related to the rates, percentage and other parameters employed by GMAC.

CHAPTER 8

Statistics and Depreciation

The following comments are intended to supplement the *Owner's Manual* and are in no way intended to conflict with that and other related HP pamphlets. The new series of HP Business Calculators have many statistical features, but the limitations of space in any *Handbook* sometimes means that only the most cursory comment can be accomodated. Readers meeting some calculations, in which they are inexperienced, may appreciate some further explanations.

Weighted mean
To take a case in point. The explanations of the extremely useful weighted mean facility are clear but they assume that users know what they want. Unhappily this is not always the case!

Most people know how to calculate an average, the sum of the data divided by the number of data items. But when there are different levels, or different bases, for various parameters then the data must be "weighted" to take the variations into consideration.

In Chapter 10, where split coupons and convertible bonds are discussed, one of the requirements is to determine the gross yield. Because there is more than one coupon, a short weighted mean calculation is necessary before the conventional calculation of (coupon x 100)/price can be executed,

Assuming that there are two coupons, one for 8% over a term of four and a half years, the other for 12% over sixteen years, the weighted mean calculation is as follows:

$$\frac{(8 \times 4.5) + (12 \times 16)}{(4.5 + 16)} = 11.121951 \text{ average coupon}$$

To input the above values into the calculator, which comes first, the percentages, or the years? Does it matter? No, but what *does* matter comes later, when you have to decide which is the X variable.

```
█ [MAIN] SUM    = ITEM(1)=?
8   [INPUT]     = ITEM(2)=?
12  [INPUT]     = ITEM(3)=?
[EXIT] NAME  Type in " CPNS " and [INPUT]
If you forget to [INPUT] the name won't register!


GET  #NEW     = ITEM(1)=?
4.5 [INPUT]     = ITEM(2)=?
16  [INPUT]     = ITEM(3)=?
[EXIT]
NAME press YRS [INPUT]  Do not forget the [INPUT]
CALC  MORE  FRCST    ON DISPLAY  CPNS  YRS  [SELECT X VARIABLE]
```

But which?

X is the bottom line of a graph and, *for a weighted mean calculation*, the X variable is the requirement. In this example the WM of the coupons is required so CPNS is the X variable and YRS the Y variable:

```
Press CPNS, press YRS , then press MORE  W.MN = 11.121951
```

If you make a mistake in input it doesn't matter, *providing* you [EXIT] [EXIT] and then repress [FRCST]. If you do not track back to [FRCST] you will get a whole lot of garbage!

The above may seem to be a somwhat lengthy process to obtain a comparatively simple weighted mean, but it must be appreciated that the facilities provided are designed for longer and more complicated problems than the two entry series above. A good example of the use of the [CFLO] facility is for the far longer type of calculation required by the "average life" example outlined in Chapter 10.

To save time, I use a short, slightly untidy program for short WM calculations like those above.

Key in the following **W/MEAN * *** program:

W/MEAN:IF(S(NEXT)   OR   S(ΣΣ):((AxB)-ΣΣ)+NEXT:(-B+Σ)-NXT)

(Ensure a space before/after OR)

| A | B | ΣΣ | NEXT | Σ | NXT |

In the example we have taken the coupons as the base variable (the X list, bottom line of the graph – the requirement is the time factor, the Y list) so first input 8 to [A]. Then input the time factor into [B].   Press [ΣΣ] to total these two values and, after pressing [INPUT], press [NEXT] which adds this result to any values previously stored. Now press [Σ] which calls forward the time factor and, after pressing [INPUT] again press [NXT] which adds this value to any values previously stored.

As I said above, untidy. But the best that can be done in the circumstances of this type of programming.

After all the entries have been entered divide the values held in the [ΣΣ] register by those held in the [Σ] register to find the weighted mean. Taking the above example:

▌ [CLEAR DATA]
This is important and must always be executed at the start of every fresh problem.

A	B	ΣΣ
8	4.5	?

            = 36 [INPUT] press   **NEXT**   **Σ**   ?
                                = 4.5 [INPUT] press **NXT**

A	B	ΣΣ
12	16	?

            = 228 [INPUT] press   **NEXT**   **Σ**   ?
                                = 20.5 [INPUT] press **NXT**

[RCL] **ΣΣ** [÷] [RCL] **Σ** [=] 11.121951 Weighted Mean.

Moving averages

For those with an inquiring mind who are not familiar with statistical calculations it may be useful to explain, briefly, how moving averages are calculated.

In the HP *Owner's Manual* the example given is to find the moving average for the number of units manufactured during the period when the totals were 4400, 5360, 2900, 3670, 4040, 3200.   The example took a *three* month moving average in order to smooth off the undoubtedly untidy line graph which the above figures would provide.

The calculated average for the second, third. and fourth months, using the [SUM] built-in program, and the HP provided MAVG program, were given as 3,976, 3,536 and 3,636 respectively. How come?

First find the average for the first three months:

(4400 + 5360 + 2900)/3 = 4,220

Now, following the *Manual* example calculations, take the fourth value (because it's a three monthly average) and subtract the first value, and divide the result by 3. Then add the sum to the last "average", namely (here) 4220:

4220.00 + ((3670 − 4400)/3) = 3,976.67
3976.67 + ((4040 − 5360)/3) = 3,536.67
3536.67 + ((3200 − 2900)/3) = 3,636.67

Using the HP program, the reader is faced with a menu display [MAVG], [LAST] and [N].

Having entered 3 in [N] and again 3 (because it's a 3 monthly average) in [LAST] pressing [MAVG] provides the first answer. Thereafter the user totally ignores [N] and keeps entering the values 4, 5, et sec. first pressing [LAST], then [MAVG].

As a purely personal comment I find this menu format slightly irritating; for quick fingering I would much prefer to commence with [LAST], followed by [MAVG], which would, to my mind, make continual input far more convenient.

Should any user be of a like mind, the HP program can easily be altered by adding   (LASTx0)+   at the beginning of the HP keyed program. The menu will now read:

LAST   MAVG   N

Exponential smoothing

Another popular method of analysing trends is the exponential smoothing method which, incidentally, belies its somewhat esoteric nomenclature, the calculations being extremely simple, quick, and needing little or no historic data.

The smoothing is executed by choosing an exponential factor of (say) 5% and employing the decimal fraction together with (1 – the decimal fraction) calculating as follows:

```
(data A x .95) + (data B x .05)  = data 1
(data 1 x .95) + (data C x .05)  = data 2
(data 2 x .95) + (data D x .05)  = data 3   and so on...
```

Employing the following data:

periods (p)	1.	2.	3.	4.	5.	6.	7.
data values	125	183	207	222	198	240	225

```
(125.00 x .95) + (183.00 x .05)  =  127.90
(127.90 x .95) + (207.00 x .05)  =  131.86 and so on...
```

Key in the following **EXP/SMOOTH** program:

EXP/SMOOTH:[1ST]x.95+[2ND]x.05=NEXT

[1ST]	[2ND]	NEXT			
125	183	?	=	127.90	[INPUT]
press	207	?	=	131.86	[INPUT]
press	222	?	=	136.36	[INPUT]
press	198	?	=	139.44	and so on...

Forecasting

Again, the limitations of space may have prevented the *Owner's Manual* from offering fuller explanation regarding the "curve fitting" of a line (HP-17B page 125, HP-19B page 162).

The one of the first actions a statistician normally takes when forecasting is to find the correlation *coefficient*; for by this method he can determine whether the data provided represents a curve or a line. The detailed calculations of how to find the coefficients can be ignored here as there are now facilities in all the HP Business Calculators to represent the various types of fitting, linear, logs, exponential and power raising.

The rule is that the [CORR] (the "fitting") should be that which is nearest to 1. If, therefore, the data was input and the coefficient for *line* showed (say) .95 and for the same data input for *curve* [EXP] the coefficient was (say) .92 the statistician would consider the data represented a line (.95 being nearer to 1 than .92) and act accordingly.

In the *Manual* example the [CORR] will be found as linear 0.90 and exponential 0.91. Thus all future calculations should treat the data provided as a *curve*, not line. But apart from the fact that the difference is minute the type of problem posed in the *Manual* example would expect a line – and conveniently so it is. But the above was mentioned "for the record".

A word of warning! Be careful not to "press a lot of buttons irrespective". If you do, in this particular program, you will obtain a host of hopelessly incorrect data. Coming from [FRCST] the display invites you to "select the X variable" (in the *Manual* example, *minutes* or *sales*). Press [MINU], being the base, the X variable, then [SALES] the Y variable. The display will show one of the fitting methods, probably [LINEAR]. Now press [CORR] and (in the *Manual* example) the display will present 0.90.

To find the coefficient for a curve [EXP] press [MORE] and then [MODL] press [EXP] [CORR] = 0.91.

Should the user want to play around with other data previously input he *must* go back, by pressing [EXIT] [EXIT] *et seq.*, until the menu line [FRCST] appears. Then restart the whole sequence of keystrokes as above. If you do not revert to [FRCST] the data will fall over!

Growth rate – line

The example in question (HP-17B, page 125 and HP-19B, page 169) is hardly a financial one, but to save the re-input of a number of various other data assume that the above data represented a company's profit figures.

To find the growth rate of a line calculation if there are six data entries:

$$100 \times [\quad (\frac{\text{6th "forecast"}}{\text{1st "forecast"}})^{1/6} \quad - 1] \quad = \text{Growth\%}$$

In this example the two calculators have a very slightly different approach in input methods, and the keying in to obtain results. Assuming, however, that the reader has obtained the [SALES] and [MINU] on display:

1 MINU press SALES   or   press 1 XLIST and YLIST (for HP-19B)
               =   802.13 [STO 0]

6 MINU press SALES   or   press 6 XLIST and YLIST (for HP-19B)
               =   2,931.50

     [÷]   [RCL 0]   [=]   3.65
▌ [y^x] 6 ▌ [1/x]   [=]   1.24
     [–] 1 [x] 100   [=]   24.11 growth rate%

Taking the same example but assuming the reader now has [SALES] and [MINU], exponential based, on display:

MINU SALES or XLIST YLIST   (for HP-19B)
   7   ?   = 4,177.40 c.f. linear forecasts outlined in both manuals

To find the exponential growth rate press [M] and multiply by 100, which in this case gives 25.28% (the nominal rate). In the circumstances of a curve fitting by exponential means (as we have here, namely continuous compounding) statisticians usuyally prefer the effective growth rate and this is easily found by: [M] ▌[MATH] ([LOG] -HP19B) [EXP] [–] 1 [x] 100 [=] 28.77%.

Depreciation While the Business Calculator *Manuals*, and
the several *Solution Books*, provide the necessary advice on
how to use the in-built depreciation programs, there is little or
no explanation of exactly how the values, derived from the
various depreciation methods shown, are calculated. But
before slightly expanding on the HP comments it may be
worth providing a perspective for UK tax requirements and at
the same time suggesting how the US-tax-orientated part of
the program, the [ACAS] menu keys, can be usefully employed
for UK calculations.

UK tax requirement reducing balance method
The UK tax system for writing down assets for tax purposes
used to be the simple one of reducing the cost by one quarter
of the asset value each year – thus achieving a complete write
off in four years.

But this method was recently changed by legislation to one of
reducing the asset value by 25% each year – which may sound
the same but isn't! For by this method the total amount
never quite disappears. This "reducing balance" method,
being peculiar to the UK is, unsurprisingly, not outlined in the
HP *Manuals*.

In the old days an office copier, costing, say, £2,000 was
written down by £500 each year until, by the end of the fourth
year, it was totally written off. But nowadays for write down
tax purposes the calculation is simply:

```
£2,000      less 25% = value end year 1.
 2,000      – 500     = £1,500
£1,500      less 25% = value end year 2.
 1,500      – 375     = £1,125
£1,125      less 25% = value end year 3.
 1,125      – 281.25 = £ 843.75
£  845.75 less 25% = value end year 4.
   845.75 – 210.94 = £ 632.81
```

– which is a very different ball-game!

By keystrokes:

```
2,000 [–] 25 [%] [=]  1,500.00
      [–] 25 [%] [=]  1,125.00
      [–] 25 [%] [=]    843.75
      [–] 25 [%] [=]    632.81
```

The value of any year can always be found from:

$$\text{cost} \times [1 - (25/100)]^y = \text{book value}$$

For example year$_4$

$$£2,000 \times [1 - (25/100)]^4 = £632.81$$

```
1 [–]  25 [%]  [=] [yˣ] 4  [x] 2000  [=]  632.81
```

The book value at the end of year 25 would be £2,000 x .75^25 = 1.51 and to write the asset value down to *one penny* would take:

$$\frac{\text{LOG} \quad .01/2000}{\text{LOG} \qquad .75} = 42.43 \text{ years}$$ Logs, LOG or LN are equally suitable

Check: $$\frac{\text{LOG} \ (632.81/2000)}{\text{LOG} \qquad .75} = 4.00 \text{ years}$$

Using the HP program

```
▌[MAIN]  FIN   DEPRC
BASIS ........ ACRS%   ACAS   (input the 25% first before 2000)
 2000           25       ?  =   500.00 [–] ▌ [LAST] = –1,500.00
–1500                    ?  =  –375.00 [–] ▌ [LAST] =  1,125.00
 1,125                   ?  =   281.25 [–] ▌ [LAST] =   –843.75
and so on...
```

The Manuals' example
The example given in the *Manuals* was for a cost of £10,000.00 [BASIS] with a scrap, [SALV], value of £500.00. The term, [LIFE], was for 5 years and we will find the three depreciation values for the *third* year.

BASIS	SALV	LIFE	ACRS%	ACRS	MORE
10,000	500	5			

YR#	FACT%	DB	SOYD	SL	MORE
3	200				

The declining balance (DB).

HP employed the declining factor (df) of 2 (double declining), although they used it as a percentage 200%

BASIS	SALV	LIFE	ACRS%	ACRS	MORE
10,000	500	5			
YR#	**FACT%**	**DB**	**SOYD**	**SL**	**MORE**
3	200	?			

```
                                              = 1,440 depreciation
                                        ↓     = 1,660 remaining value
          Cost  x (1 − df÷n)^y−1 x df÷n = depreciation for year₃
          10,000 x (1 −  2÷5)^2   x  2÷5 = 1,440.00
          (10,000 x (1 −  2÷5)^3)  − 500 = 1,660.00 book value year₃
```

The straight line (SL) method

This is conceptually simple and is usually employed when the asset is not expected to depreciate greatly over the short term – it is applied to warehouses, buildings and property in general.

BASIS	SALV	LIFE	ACRS%	ACRS	MORE
10,000	500	5			
YR#	**FACT%**	**DB**	**SOYD**	**SL**	**MORE**
3	ignore			?	

```
(FACT% only applicable to DB Calc:)      = 1,900 depreciation
                                    ↓     = 3,800 remaining value
                  (Cost − salvage)÷n = depreciation each year
                      (10,000 − 500)÷5 = 1,900
         (10,000 − 500) − (1,900 x 3) = 3,800 book value year₃
```

The sum of the years' digits (SOYD) method

BASIS	SALV	LIFE	ACRS%	ACRS	MORE
10,000	500	5			
YR#	**FACT%**	**DB**	**SOYD**	**SL**	**MORE**
3	ignore		?		

```
                                              = 1,900 depreciation
                                        ↓     = 1,900 remaining value
(Cost − scrap) x ((n − y) + 1)/SOYD  (where SOYD = (n+(n+1))/2
                                                  = (5+6)/2 = 15)
      (10,000 − 500) x ((5 − 3) + 1)/15  = 1,900 depreciation year₃
          1,900/2 x (5 − 3)              = 1,900 book value year₃
```

For demonstration purposes each type of depreciation was taken separately. In practice, of course, once the data had been input it would merely be a matter of pressing just the three keys, one after the other, [DB], [SOYD] and [SL] and taking the last menu line:

YR#	FACT%	DB	SOYD	SL	MORE
3	200	?	?	?	
		=1,440	=1,900	=1,900	

Don't forget to re-input 200 to [FACT%]

Modified IRR and Financial Management RR

In the latest HP-17B/19B and HP-27S *Real Estate, Banking and Leasing Solutions* books an example was taken which had three IRRs – and consequently none were of value! The reason for the multitude of answers was because this example had several cash flows, both positive and negative – as would not be unusual with real estate cash flows which include rentals (+), upkeep (–), tax (–) etc:.

The example is repeated below – with some material concerning MIRR calculations.

Modified IRR

The example mentioned above was:

Months	Cash flows
1	−180,000
5	100,000
5	−100,000
9	zero
1	200,000

and putting this data into the [CFLO] discipline:

```
[EXIT]  FIN   CFLO   █ [CLEAR DATA]    CLEAR THE LISTS?   [YES]
FLOW(0)=?    -180000  [INPUT]
FLOW(1)=?     100000  [INPUT]
#TIMES(1)=1        5  [INPUT]
FLOW(2)=?    -100000  [INPUT]
#TIMES(2)=1        5  [INPUT]
FLOW(3)=?          0  [INPUT]
#TIMES(3)=1        9  [INPUT]
FLOW(4)=?     200000  [INPUT]
#TIMES(4)=1           [INPUT]
FLOW(5)=?
[EXIT]  CALC   IRR  = MANY/NO SOLUTIONS: KEY IN GUESS: [STO]  IRR
1   [STO]  [IRR]    = 1.86
15  [STO]  [IRR]    = 14.35
30  [STO]  [IRR]    = 29.02
```

Which is not overly helpful to the statistician!

When a project contains several alternative positive and
negative cash flows the calculations and resulting answers can
be adversely affected. But this should in no way lead to lack
of confidence in DCF disciplines in general, or in the HP
in-built [CFLO] program in particular, for it must be
remembered that the example mentioned above is unusual
and hardly likely to be met in normal circumstances.

The reason why the conventional method fails here, providing
three useless answers, is that the whole concept of discounted
cash flow calculations assumes that as interest is engendered
it is *automatically reinvested at the internal rate of return* – and
with several positive and negative cash flows this assumption
is put at risk.

Furthermore, when dealing in real estate cash flows, rentals,
income (+), and tax and upkeep, outgoings (–), can be
accurately forecast; and the absurd situation often arises in
which the IRR is (say) 25% when everyone knows that in real
life any liquidity invested would only obtain the "going rate"of
interest, probably many points below 25%!

A conventional method of overcoming this difficulty is to discount the negative cash flows at a "safe" rate (say around the UK bank rate, or US prime rate) whereas the positive cash flows can be discounted at a "risk" or entrepreneurial rate, say between 15 and 25%. This eliminates the sign change and consequently the possibility of several answers.

The example above could be calculated as follows, taking the HP's example safe rate as 8% and a risk rate of 13%:

```
[EXIT]  █ [CLEAR DATA]  CLEAR THE LISTS? [YES]
FLOW(0)=?    -180000  [INPUT]
FLOW(1)=?       0     [INPUT]
#TIMES(1)=1  5        [INPUT]
FLOW(2)=?    -100000  [INPUT]
#TIMES(2)=1  5        [INPUT]
FLOW(3)=?    [EXIT]   [CALC] 8 ÷ 12 [I%] [NPV] = -654,136.81 [STO 0]


[EXIT]  █ [CLEAR DATA]  CLEAR THE LISTS? [YES]
FLOW(0)=?    0        [INPUT]
FLOW(1)=?    100000   [INPUT]
#TIMES(1)=1  5        [INPUT]
FLOW(2)=?    0        [INPUT]
#TIMES(2)=1  14       [INPUT]
FLOW(3)=?    200000   [INPUT]
#TIMES(3)=1  [EXIT]   [CALC] 13 ÷ 12 [I%] [NFV] =  800,582.75 [STO 1]


█ [MAIN]   FIN    TVM    OTHER    12   P/YR   END    [EXIT]
     N     I%YR   PV     PMT      FV   OTHER
    20      ?    [RCL0]    0    [RCL1]
          = 12.18 MIRR
```

Now for the good news!

In the HP *Real Estate Solutions* book mentioned above there is an excellent and extremely sophisticated program which makes all those calculations unnecessary – at least for 17B/19B users. (HP-27S users will, unhappily, need to use the calculations outlined above.) A copy of the program, slightly altered for menu presentation, is given below.

Key in the following **MIRR** program:

```
MIRR:SGN(SAFE)xSGN(RISK)x(1+MIRR÷100)^Σ(L
:1:SIZEC(INV):1:#T(INV:L))=-Σ(J:0:SIZEC(I
NV):1:MAX(FLOW(INV:J):0)xUSFV(RISK:#T(INV
:J))xSPFV(RISK:Σ(L:J+1:SIZEC(INV):1:#T(IN
V:L))))÷(MIN(FLOW(INV:0):0)+Σ(J:1:SIZEC(I
NV):1:MIN(FLOW(INV:J):0)xUSPV(SAFE:#T(INV
:J))xSPPV(SAFE:Σ(L:1:J-1:1:#T(INV:L)))))
```

> SAFE   RISK   MIRR

When using the program the cash flows must first be keyed-in to the [CFLO] discipline and the name chosen *must* be the same as that written into the formula above, namely "INV". If this is inconvenient and another name is required then the program must be adjusted accordingly.

```
█ [MAIN]  FIN   CFLO
CLEAR THE LIST?          YES
ALSO CLEAR LIST NAME     YES
FLOW(0)=?
180000 [+/-] [INPUT]
FLOW(1)=?
100000       [INPUT]
#TIMES(1)=1
5            [INPUT]
FLOW(2)=?
100000 [+/-] [INPUT]
TIMES#(2)=1
5            [INPUT]
FLOW(3)=?
0            [INPUT]
#TIMES(3)=1
9            [INPUT]
FLOW(4)=?
200000       [INPUT]
#TIMES(4)=1  [INPUT]
[EXIT] NAME
TYPE A NAME; [INPUT]
INV          [INPUT]
```

Reverting to the MIRR program:

```
█ [MAIN]  SOLVE    ↑↓   MIRR  CALC
  SAFE     RISK    MIRR
  8/12    13/12     ?           =  1.01523 MONTHLY MIRR
                          [x] 12 = 12.182830  MIRR (see above)
```

Do not forget, when using the program, that in the above example the compounding was monthly so the [SAFE] and [RISK] rates must be input in their monthly rate format and the resulting [MIRR] must be multiplied by 12 before presenting the nominal rate%.

When a mix is a must

In DCF calculations it is necessary for all the cash flows to retain their constant term flow, namely annually, monthly, quarterly, weekly or even daily. As no "mix" is permissible, what happens if one has a case of monthly income and, say, quarterly tax outgoings? For cash flows over a number of years it just is not practicable to work on a monthly basis with (say) 3 months of £x income and 1 month of tax outgoings repeated over, say, 25 years.

So sometimes a mix is a must and, within reason, the constant term flow limitation mentioned above can be circumvented. For instance suppose that we had income of £135 per month and taxes to pay of £150 each quarter. If the term was for 10 years, and the IRR is 10% nominal, what is the Net Present Value (NPV), namely the "cost" of the investment?

What we can do is to calculate the balance of the positive income and then deduct the outgoings – having first converted the monthly/quarterly *interest* rate to a common (*effective*) base.

Obviously, if the respective cash flows above were uneven a DCF calculation would be necessary.   But in the above example, as the cash flows are even, the [TVM] discipline can be used.

N	I%YR	PV	PMT	FV	OTHER 12 P/YR	END	[EXIT]
120	10	?	−135	0	PV = 10,215.61	[STO1]	

[EXIT] ICONV	PER						
NOM	EFF	P					
10	?	12	= 10.47 effective				
NOM	EFF	P					
?	10.47	4	= 10.08 nominal [STO 2]				

[EXIT] [EXIT] TVM							
N	I%YR	PV	PMT	FV	OTHER 4 P/YR	[EXIT]	<--
40	[RCL2]	?	−150	0			
				= 3,752.20			

[−]   [RCL 1]   [=]   [+/−] = 6,463.40 Investment cost

By equation:

135a_____   at (10/12)%   −   150a_____   at (10.083565/4)

    120 | 40 |

  10,215.61   −   3,752,20   =   6,463.40

A further study of MIRR and FMRRs can be made from Financial Calculations for Business *by Christian de Lisle and a pamphlet* Finance and Taxation Techniques *by Messner (obtained from Realtor's National Marketing Institute of Chicago).*

The beta coefficient

The age-old argument over whether investment decisions are best made by "feel", experience and knowledge of a particular market, or by various "measurement of risk" formulae will probably never be fully resolved.   In the States, where "flying by the seat of one's pants" plays little or no part in investment policy, there is a plethora of risk formulae of every kind and description.   One such is the beta coefficient measure of market risk.   This method considers the dispersion of the value around the mean value resulting from the general ebb and flow of market fluctuations: the stock or portfolio being compared to an index of choice.

The beta, therefore, is a measure of risk of a stock or portfolio. When the beta coefficient equals 0 the rate of return is considered to be "without risk"; whereas a beta of 1 equates to the normal investment risk in a diversified portfolio of stocks. The higher the beta, above 1, the greater the assumed risk.

Comparisons are made between a "riskless" market investment, such as, in the States, a short dated US Treasury Bill and rate of return as shown by an index of choice, such as, in the States, the Standard & Poor's 500.

An example of a beta calculation is given in the excellent Hewlett-Packard applications book, *Personal Investment and Tax Planning"*.

Given that the anticipated annual return of a stock is 15%, if the current risk-free yield on a US 91-day T Bill is 5.52% and the estimated return on the Standard & Poor's 500 index is 13.25%, what is the beta coefficient of the stock in question?

The short formula is:

$$\frac{\text{Yield\% } - \text{ T Bill rate\%}}{\text{Index\% } - \text{ T Bill rate\%}} = \text{Beta}$$

$$\frac{15 \ - \ 5.52}{13.25 \ - \ 5.52} = 1.23$$

The premium paid for the above risk is, of course, simply the risk value (the index rate) minus the riskless value (the T Bill), here $13.25 - 5.52 = 7.73$ premium.

To estimate the beta of a complete portfolio requires the summation of various data, related to the number of shares in the portfilio. In the above-mentioned applications book there is a comprehensive example, with an excellent program provided, and a full explanation of the required method of calculation.

CHAPTER 9

Bonds - Prices and Yields to Maturity

General
The HP Business Calculators are supplied with a complete set of in-built bond programs provided to determine US corporate bonds (30/360 semi-annual), US Treasury bonds (actual semi-annual) and Eurobonds (30/360 annual or semi-annual). A program is provided below for various UK methods of calculation. Many statisticians will doubtless wish to acquire one or other of the calculators for these comprehensive facilities alone.

Yields to maturity (YTM)
The gross yield on a normal investment is the annual interest multiplied by 100 and divided by the cost (price): 10% x 100 ÷ £90 = 11.11% But when the investment is one where the borrower guarantees not only to pay interest annually but also to repay the original stake when the investment matures, it becomes a different ball game.

Consider: if a bond could be bought in the market place for a cost of, say, £80 with £100 being repaid in 10 years' time, then, mathematically, ignoring any fluctuations of the market the capital value of the investment will gain 20 points in 10 years - or 2 points each year. In that case the conventional gross yield measurement would hardly be a useful investment criterion. What is obviously required is a calculation which will add the capital lift between purchase and maturity to the normal gross yield. This is the "yield to maturity" - referred to, in the pages that follow, as the YTM%. But in the menu driven programs provided below, the YTM will be referred to as the YLD% because this is the nomenclature employed by HP in their in-built bond programs.

The actuarial formula

The basic concept of discounting the redemption value, and each periodic payment, back to settlement applies to all bonds. Any differences in the various methods of calculation apply, not to the main concept, but to some of the peripheral factors, varying with the type of "calendar" used and the accrued interest due, for example:

$$\frac{RV(1 + i/p)^{-n} + Da_{\overline{n}|} + D}{(1 + i/p)^k} = DP$$

For Simple interest calculations the denominator is $1 + (i/p \times k)$

DP   = Dirty Price, namely Clean Price + Accrued Interest

Where:
the "actuarial amortisation" equals

$$a_{\overline{n}|} = (1 - (1 + i/p)^{-n})/(i/p)$$

i   = the YTM% as a decimal
         If 10% = YTM then $i = 10/100 = 0.10$
p   = periods per year
         If semi-annual p = 2 (i/p at 10% = $10/200 = 0.05$)

RV   = Redemption Value, called the "call" by HP and others
D   = the half coupon for semi-annual calculations
         $(n + k)$ = the total number of days between settlement
         and maturity (less any leap days) divided by "base"

Base   = 365   for "actual" calendar
               semi-annual 182.5, 181, 182, 183, 184 (dependent)
         360   for   30/360
               semi-annual 180

Take the simple example of a US corporate bond with a life of 5000 days. 5000 when divided by 360 = 13.888888 and for semi annual interest payments equals an $(n + k)$ of 27.777778, namely 27 half years (n) and .7777 (k) x 180 = 140 odd days between settlement date and the next payment date.

Assuming the coupon was 10% nominal, the YTM 11% and the RV 100:

$$\frac{(100 \times 1.055^{-27}) + (5 \times (1 - 1.055^{-27})/.055) + 5}{1.055^{\,0.7777}} =$$

$$\frac{23.560450 \quad + \quad 69.490500 \quad + \quad 5}{1.042522} = DP$$

$$= \$94.052$$

```
(1 - k)        x    coupon  =  accrued interest
(1 - .888889)  x      10    =     1.11111
```

consequently the *clean* price, that is the *quoted* price, equals 94.052 – 1.11111 = $92.94

The Hewlett-Packard bond program

Employing the calculator's bond program, 5000 days from a settlement date, [SETT], of January 1, 1987 gives a maturity date, [MAT], of November 21, 2000, employing the financial calendar (30/360):

```
▌ [MAIN]  FIN    BOND    TYPE   360    SEMI  [EXIT]
  TYPE   SETT    MAT     CPN%   CALL   MORE
       1.011987 11.212000  10   (100)
  YLD%  PRICE   ACCRU                  MORE
   11     ?
          = 92.940569
```

```
[+] ACCRU [=] (on display) 92.94569 + 1.111111 [=] 94.051680
namely,                    price + accrued   = dirty price
```

The [CALL] register defaults to 100 but advises if altered. The accrued interest, [ACCRU], is *automatically* calculated to full precision (12 sig.fig.) and is, therefore, *non-adjustable.*

Eurobonds

All calculations of Eurobonds are governed by the rules of the Association of International Bond Dealers (AIBD). Rule 226 states specifically that the *accrued interest will always be rounded to two places of decimals*. Because the HP bond program does not round the accrued interest, officially, Eurobonds should not be calculated on this HP program! In practice, as the only difference in calculation between US corporate bonds and Eurobonds is the rounding, it is hardly surprising that the same computer programs are usually employed to calculate both classes of bonds - the Euro rounding requirement, if known (!), being conveniently ignored! The difference is insignificant; the clean price above, with the a/i unrounded, is 92.941, whereas if correctly Euro rounded it is 92.942.

Eurobonds are annual interest paid but if, following a country of origin practice, semi-annual calculations are required the YTM must converted to its effective rate e.g., 10% becomes 10.25% and is marked (S). To find a price from a YTM%(S) first convert to its nominal profile, then divide by 2 for the i/p.

AIBD Rule 224(2) states that if maturity should fall on the 31st of any month (or the 28th or 29th of February) the date for maturity, and thus the affected anniversary periodic payments, will always be treated as if it was the 30th of the month. As US corporate bonds have the same requirement no problem arises when calculating Eurobonds on the HP program, the rule being part of the program.

US Treasury bonds

Conversely, for "T" bonds, as outlined in the HP *Owner's Manual*, in Appendix B under "Bond Calculations", if maturity falls on the last day of the month, then the *coupon payments* will also fall on the last day of the month. For example, if maturity falls on September 30, the coupon payments will be on March 31 and September 30.

The formula and short explanation provides little help in understanding precisely how US Treasury bonds are calculated - unlike the somewhat more comprehensive guidance given in previous HP *Manuals*.

In short, the actuarial method, outlined above, for semi–annual coupon bonds, divides the total number of days between settlement and maturity by 182.5, or 180 depending on the calendar used, to provide the (n + k). This factor is the number of half years in the life of the bond (the "n" factor) and the number of odd days between settlement date and the next payment date (the "k" factor).

The US T Bond is calculated slightly differently, employing a usage which is sometimes known as the *quasi-coupon period* method. In this case the (n + k) is the number of half year periods (n) in the life of the bond plus the number of odd days (k) divided, *not* by 182.5, but by the number of days in the coupon period in which settlement occurs. Obviously, this divisor will be 181,182,183 or 184, depending in which part of the year the dates occur. The accrued interest becomes the half coupon multiplied by (1 – k). The number of odd days and the a/i days, *include any intervening leap days.*

Japanese "averaging formula"
Using the actuarial formula/equation, the price can be found without much difficulty, but without a computer program the interpolation required to find the yield is a little too cumbersome to be attractive. The Japanese method needs no aids, save the back of the proverbial envelope, and consequently can be extremely useful as a rough check on many such calculations.

$$\left[cpn + \frac{(call - clean\ price) \times 365}{life\ in\ days} \right] \times \frac{call}{clean\ price} = Yield\%$$

$$\frac{(cpn \times call/yield\%) + (365 \times call/life\ days \times call/yield\%)}{(call/yield\% \times 365/life\ days) + 1} = Price$$

The life is usually assumed not to include leap days, and while it is customary to calculate on an "actual" (365) basis there is no reason why the 30/360 calendar cannot be used if required.

Assume a price of 92.941, coupon 10%, call 100, and a life of 5,000 days (financial calendar) the YTM equals:

100 [–] 92.941 [x] 360 [÷] 5000 [+] 10 [x] 100 [÷] 92.941 [=] 11.306

Key in the following **JAP** program:

```
JAP:YLD%xSGN(PRICE)xSGN(CPN)=SGN(N)x(CPN+
((CALL-PRICE)÷N))xCALL÷PRICE
```

YLD%	PRICE	CPN	N	CALL	
11	?	10	5000/360	100	PRICE=94.505
	?		5069/365		PRICE=94.506
	?		* 5073/365		PRICE=94.504
			* (leap days included)		

An all-purpose bond formula
The in-built HP bond program, when 365 and semi-annually based, calculates only by the quasi-coupon periods method mentioned above, which, while perhaps being the most accurate of all methods, differs from those employed by the London market.

While the UK bond market also bases its calculations on semi-annual coupon payments, employing the 365 calendar, the days-life of a bond is divided by 182.5 to find the number of payment periods and the odd days – unlike the quasi-coupon period method where the days-base is the number of days in the coupon period.

The statistician, while normally using the date method entry to calculate the life of the bond, more often than not needs to make various peripheral calculations – which employ the number of days between settlement and maturity, settlement and the previous payment date, and sometimes settlement and the next payment date.

The all-purpose program below is designed to assist both the investment user and the dedicated statistician by permitting the life of the bond to be input *either* as a date entry *or* the number of days between settlement and maturity.

Key in the following **BONDS** program:

```
BONDS:SGN(YLD%)xPRICE+0xSETT+0xMAT+IF(FP(
A/DTEx100)=0:A/DTE:DDAYS(A/DTE:SETT+0xMAT
:IF(BASE=360:3:1)))÷BASExCPN=IF(CPN<>0:+(
((SPPV(YLD%÷P:INT(IF(FP(SETTx100)=0:SETT:
DDAYS(SETT:MAT:IF(BASE=360:3:2)))÷BASExP)
))xCALL)+    CPN÷P    —IF(XD=1:CPN÷P:0)+CPN
÷PxUSPV(YLD%÷P:INT(IF(FP(SETTx100)=0:SETT
:DDAYS(SETT:MAT:IF(BASE=360:3:2)))÷BASExP
)))xIF(SINT=1:(1÷(1+YLD%÷P÷100xFP(IF(FP(S
ETTx100)=0:SETT:DDAYS(SETT:MAT:IF(BASE=36
0:3:2)))÷BASExP))):SPPV(YLD%÷P:FP(IF(FP(S
ETTx100)=0:SETT:DDAYS(SETT:MAT:IF(BASE=36
0:3:2)))÷BASExP))):CALLxSPPV(YLD%÷P:IF(FP
(SETTx100)=0:SETT:DDAYS(SETT:MAT:IF(BASE=
360:3:2)))÷BASExP))
```

YLD%	PRICE	SETT	MAT	A/DTE	MORE
BASE	CPN	P	CALL	XD	MORE
SINT					

User instructions

All entries are made in their *nominal* format, annual YTM or coupon. The [P] label, with an input of 1 or 2, controls whether the calculation is annual or semi-annual.

The program defaults to zero in labels [XD] and [SINT]. For an ex-dividend calculation, *or when bonds are at issue,* enter 1 to [XD]. If simple interest discounting is required input 1 to [SINT]. As the [CALL] label also defaults to zero the requisite call value should always be checked for each new calculation.

The base, for the life of the bond, is either 365 or 360 (although even these value are occasionally subject to "adjustment") and is input to [BASE]. The life itself can be input either by the dates for settlement to [SETT], maturity to [MAT], and the accrued interest days to [A/DTE]; or just the number of days between settlement and maturity to [SETT] with the number of a/i days to [A/DTE].

The program is designed to ignore any leap days intervening in the number of the days between settlement and maturity, but, if necessary for statistical purposes, this limitation can be circumvented, as outlined in some examples below..

The box [A/DTE] is the register which holds the value, be it the the *days* between or the *date* for, the coupon payment date *prior* to settlement day (for cum-div) and/or the date *after* settlement day (for ex-div calculations).

Even if employing the date entry method the number of a/i days can, if required, be input to [A/DTE]. On occasions the number of days will be. for some calculations, zero or a number of days plus a fraction of a day. Such values can be input to both [SETT] and [A/DTE] *providing* the decimals do not exceed two places. It will be seen, later, that being able to mix days and dates can prove extremely valuable.

Providing that [SETT] and [A/DTE] hold either dates or days, given the YTM, the price found is the clean price; whereas if 0 is keyed into [A/DTE] the price found will be the quoted price *plus* the accrued interest, the dirty price. It will be appreciated, therefore, that to subtract the clean price from the dirty price will result in the accrued interest.

If it is proposed, in due course, to find the duration or volatility values, transferring to the DURATION program (see later), the life input method used must be days, not dates.

Should "BAD GUESSES" ever display check the *date* entry!

Example: Taking the HP Bond program example above, which was both worked through by equation and calculated on the HP in-built 360 semi-annual discipline: settlement was January 1, 1987 (1.011987) and maturity November 21, 2000 (11.212000). Thus the payment date prior to settlement must be November 21, 1986.

Employing the 360 calendar the "days between" (settlement and maturity) will be found as 5000, and the accrued interest days will be 5000/360 [–] 14 [=] [+/–] [x] 360 [=] 40 days.

Assume a YTM% of 11%, a call of 100, and a coupon of 10%, which gives an accrued interest of 40 x 10 ÷ 360 = 1.1111111.

Input the above values to the BONDS program to find the price:

YLD%	PRICE	SETT	MAT	A/DTE	MORE
11	?	1.011987	11.212000	11.211986	

BASE	CPN	P	CALL	XD	MORE
360	10	2	100	0	

SINT					PRICE = 92.94
0					clean [STO 0]

YLD%	PRICE	SETT	MAT	A/DTE	MORE
11	?	1.011987	11.212000	**0**	

BASE	CPN	P	CALL	XD	MORE
360	10	2	100	0	

SINT					PRICE = 94.05
0					dirty

94.05 − [RCL 0] = 1.111111 a/i

The same answers can be found by using the "days between" method

YLD%	PRICE	SETT	MAT	A/DTE	MORE
11	?	5000		40	

BASE	CPN	P	CALL	XD	MORE
360	10	2	100	0	

SINT					PRICE = 92.94
					clean

YLD%	PRICE	SETT	MAT	A/DTE	MORE
11	?	5000		**0**	

BASE	CPN	P	CALL	XD	MORE
360	10	2	100	0	

SINT					PRICE = 94.05
					dirty

A personal date program

It will be appreciated that, when not using the dates input method, the number of "days between" must be found – and to find "days between" a program must be employed. If the HP program [TIME], [CALC], [DATE1], [DATE2] discipline is used the inevitable switching between the [SOLVE] program and the HP program becomes both cumbersome and tedious.

As a result, it is suggested that the following short date program be kept just above or below the keyed-in BONDS program so that the switch between the two programs is simplified.

The values are *not* shared with other programs, so dates can be calculated without other data being affected.

Key in the following **DATES** program:

```
DATES:DDAYS(DATE1:DATE2:IF(#?#=1:1:IF(#?#
=2:2:IF(#?#=3:3:3))))=DAYS
```

DATE1	DATE2	#?#	DAYS	
[INPUT]	to	#?#	1	for ACTual dates (365)
"	"	"	2	" ACTual dates (365) less leap days
"	"	"	3	" 30/360 dates

From an earlier example, input the two following dates: 1.011987 and 11.212000:

DATE1	DATE2	#?#	DAYS	
1.011987	11.212000	3	?	= 5,000 days

Alternatively:

DATE1	DATE2	#?#	DAYS	
7.041988	?	1	174	= Christmas Day!

Zero coupon bonds

Taking the HP *Manuals'* example of a zero-coupon bond, namely a semi-annual bond, based 30/360, purchased May 19, 1986 with maturity June 30, 2000 and a yield to maturity of 10%, find the price, which in the example is given as 25.23. The 30/360 "days between" is 5081 days.

YLD%	PRICE	SETT	MAT	A/DTE	MORE
10	?	5.191986	6.302000	12.311985	

BASE	CPN	P	CALL	XD	MORE
365	0	2	100	0	

SINT					
0				PRICE = 25.227440	

(Remember, on page 129, the end month rule.)

A Canadian Treasury strip bond, another word for a zero coupon bond, with an interest rate of 11½% and a redemption value of Cdn$ 2,040 on September 1, 2005. The price of the bond, at settlement, on September 9, 1987 is Cdn$ 288. If the amount purchased is Cdn$ 130,000 what is the realisation at maturity?

Canada uses the 365 calendar, thus there are 6562 days between settlement and redemption (excluding leap days).

YLD%	PRICE	SETT	MAT	A/DTE	MORE
?	288	6562			

BASE	CPN	P	CALL	XD	MORE
365	0	2	2040	0	

SINT
0

YLD% = 11.191533

As the actual cost of the bargain was Cdn$ 130,000 the realisation at maturity is:

YLD%	PRICE	SETT	MAT	A/DTE	MORE
11.1915	130000	6562			

BASE	CPN	P	CALL	XD	MORE
365	0	2	?	0	

SINT
0

Realisation (call) = Cdn$ 920,833.33

It should not be thought that because there is no coupon, and therefore no annual income, the benefit is solely a matter of capital gains – which may or may not be taxed at maturity.

For the taxation of zero or strip bonds is peculiar to the revenue requirements of individual countries. In Canada, for example, there is no capital gains tax but tax is levied on the assessed interest *every three years* and, therefore, in the above example the assessment will be 130,000 x 11.5/100 x 3 = Cdn$ 44,850 in year three. This sum would be added to the other annual income of the bond holder and tax for that year would be assessed accordingly.

Average life - sinking funds - calculations

Some institutional borrowers sometimes partially redeem their issues at various stages during the life of the bond. In such cases the YTM% are of limited value.

The calculations require the exact structure of each redemption amount and the date when it was effected. This means not only checking back to the details of the original loan but also any interim arrangements. For while the redemption dates and values, once notified, cannot be rescinded there is nothing to stop the companies increasing their redemption amounts if so desired. Such changes are published from time to time in the financial press. The resulting weighted mean value, found by the HP SUM program, becomes the (n + k) factor in the conventional actuarial formula/equation.

Example: Assume a 20 million Eurodollar issued December 15, 1969 with maturity 20 years later. The redemption dates and amounts are: 1978 & 1979, $500,000.   1980 - 1986 (incl), $1,000,000. 1987 & 1988, $1,250,000 and in 1989 (some 20 years after issue) the residual will be repaid to holders.

The method is to work backwards from maturity, and so the first value to determine is the residual, namely:

```
20 - ((1.25M x 2yrs) + (1M x 7yrs) + (.5M x 2 yrs)) = $9.50M.
```

Repayment amount	Year	No. Years to Issue Date
$ 9,500,000	1989	20
1,250,000	1988	19
1,250,000	1987	18
1,000,000	1986	17
1,000,000	1985	16
1,000,000	1984	15
1,000,000	1983	14
1,000,000	1982	13
1,000,000	1981	12
1,000,000	1980	11
500,000	1979	10
500,000	1978	9

No capital repayments made before 1978

Finding the (n + k) factor:

▌ [MAIN] SUM   GET   #NEW ITEM(1)=? displays.
Key in 20 [INPUT], then 19 [INPUT] and so on until 9 has been input.
After last entry ITEM(13)=? will display.
Press [EXIT]   NAME If not already registered, type in YRS and [INPUT].
(don't forget the [INPUT] *or the name won't register).*
[EXIT] [EXIT] [EXIT] GET   #NEW ITEM(1)=? displays:
key in 9.5 [INPUT] then 1.25 [INPUT], and so on until the last .5 entry
has been input. ITEM(13)=? will then display:
[EXIT] NAME and type in PMTS [INPUT] [EXIT] CALC   MORE
FRCST displaying PMTS and YRS

Note The above keystrokes are as per HP-17B. Those for the
HP-19B are slightly different.

Which to press first? A wrong decision will result in a totally
incorrect answer! For weighted mean calculations the tip is to
press the requirement first. Here the answer required is the
average life, which is in years – so press years [YRS]:

YRS PMTS MORE W.MN = 17.1875 (n + k) with an annual profile.

If settlement occurred on December 15, 1977 rather than at
issue, the calculation for [YRS] must be redone but the [PMTS]
can stand (see schedule):

[EXIT] [EXIT] [EXIT] SUM   GET   YRS ▌ [CLEAR DATA]
CLEAR THE LIST? YES ALSO CLEAR LIST NAME? NO

Key in 12 [INPUT] 11 [INPUT] and so on until 1 has been input:

[EXIT] CALC   MORE   FRCST   YRS   PMTS   MORE   W.MN = 9.1875 (n + k)

Settlement after partial payments have commenced
If settlement occurs after some of the capital has already been
redeemed the calculation requires dates/days between
settlement and maturity.

If, for example, the above 10% Eurobond was traded at a
quoted price (clean) of 99 with settlement May 29, 1984
and the YTM is 10.216%, what is the average life yield?

First check the YTM%:

[EXIT]	[EXIT]	SOLVE ↓↑	BONDS	CALC	
YLD%	PRICE	SETT	MAT	A/DTE	MORE
?	99	5.291984	12.151989	12.151983	
BASE	CPN	P	CALL	XD	MORE
360	10	1	100	0	
SINT				YLD% =10.216	

There are 1996 days between settlement and maturity, therefore the (n + k) is 1996/360 = 5.54444 and consequently the a/i is 10 x (1 – .54444) = 4.55556 or 4.56 (AIBD rounded).

To find the YTM, *correct to the AIBD rounded a/i*, calculate as follows:

4.56 + 99 = 103.56 PRICE key-in 0 A/DTE press YLD% = 10.214
or 4.56 ÷ 10 x 360 = 164.16 press A/DTE press YLD% = 10.214

In average life calculations the life of a bond is found in terms of the (n + k), and the advantage of being able to input a number of days, plus a fractional day, soon becomes apparent.

Example continued: With the above requirement and the schedule below find the [W.MN], namely the (n + k) factor:

Repayment amount	Year	Years to Issue Date
$ 9,500,000	1989	5.54444444
1,250,000	1988	4.54444444
1,250,000	1987	3.54444444
1,000,000	1986	2.54444444
1,000,000	1985	1.54444444

■ [MAIN] SUM GET YRS ■ [CLEAR DATA] CLEAR LIST? YES
ALSO CLEAR LIST NAME ? NO
[INPUT] 5.5444444, 4.544444, 3.544444 et sec: until ITEM(6)? displays:
[EXIT] GET PMTS ■ [CLEAR DATA] CLEAR THE LIST? YES
ALSO CLEAR LIST NAME? NO 9.5 [INPUT] 1.25 [INPUT] 1.25 [INPUT] 1
[INPUT] 1 [INPUT] [EXIT] CALC MORE FRCST YRS PMTS MORE
W.MN = 4.776587 (n + k) [STO 0]

(Again the keystrokes for the HP-19B differ slightly).

Reverting to the BONDS program: 4.776587 x 360 = 1,719.571320 and so, remembering the 2 decimal place limitation, input 1719.57 to [SETT].

The accrued interest days 4.776587 [–] 5 [=] [+/–] x 360 [=] 80.428680, so input 80.43 to [A/DTE]:

YLD%	PRICE	SETT	MAT	A/DTE	MORE
?	99	1719.57		80.43	
BASE	CPN	P	CALL	XD	MORE
360	10	1	100	0	
SINT					
0				= 10.252% Average Life Yield	

Duration and volatility
The duration of a loan is the weighted average of the life of the bond; the mean of the number of payment periods, which (except for zero coupon bonds) is always shorter than the normal [n + k] term of the loan. Because of the natural market fluctuations, the loan duration is sometimes considered to be a useful measurement of the risk factor. Indeed some, but by no means all, consider that it is a better benchmark than the conventional YTM%.

The duration value must be determined first if volatility is required; for the volatility is merely the duration value divided by 1 + (YTM% ÷ (p x 100)).

The volatility calculation, or elasticity as it is sometimes called, can be used to determine the new price of a bond after an increase or decrease of the YTM%. Although the resulting prices are not precise they are reasonably accurate and for a quick listing can often save the labour of a full calculation.

There are two ways of calculating the new prices using the volatility factor, depending on how you address the latter calculation. For the change in YTM values can be expressed either as the difference between the old and new values or as an increased or decreased percentage.

```
Expressed as a difference, duration ÷ (1 + i/p)          = volatility
Expressed as a percentage, duration ÷ (1 + i/p) x (i/p) = volatility
```

The duration programs

In the HP *Personal Investment and Tax Planning Applications* book, page 122, a duration program is provided which is only accurate for bonds at issue, or with no "odd days". Consequently this limits the use of the program.

The duration calculation is one of discounting each payment period and takes into account the call or redemption amount: in all a fairly simple schedule and one which, with a moderately short program, can easily be executed on the HP-12C calculator. For the HP-12C has a conventional step by step method of programming. But, unhappily, the method employed by both the HP-17B and 19B, does not lend itself to the framing of a schedule. I am, therefore, much indebted to Dr David Branston, the senior partner of the software consultants, Deltasoft Ltd (with whom I was then collaborating to produce a series of spread sheet "Bond Yield" programs for 4-5-6 World Ltd), for suggesting the use of geometric progression as an alternative to scheduling. For without this ingenious idea and his invaluable help, I should not have been able to construct the program below.

Key in the following **DURATION * *** program:

```
DURATION:IF(S(YLD%)  OR  S(DUR):SGN(YLD%)
xSGN(CPN)xSGN(P)x(((YLD%÷P÷100+1)^-INT(SE
TT÷BASExP))xCALLxSETT÷BASExP+(CPN÷P)÷(1-I
NV(YLD%÷P÷100+1))x((FP(SETT÷BASExP)-((YLD
%÷P÷100+1)^-(INT(SETT÷BASExP)+1))xSETT÷BA
SExP)+(1-(YLD%÷P÷100+1)^-(INT(SETT÷BASExP
)+1)x(YLD%÷P÷100+1))÷(1-INV(YLD%÷P÷100+1)
)x(INV(YLD%÷P÷100+1)))-IF(XD=1:((CPN÷PxFP
(SETT÷BASExP))):0))÷(((1÷(1-(1÷(YLD%÷P÷10
0+1))))xCPN÷P)x(1-(YLD%÷P÷100+1)^-(INT(SE
TT÷BASExP)+1))+(CALLx(1+(YLD%÷P÷100))^-IN
T(SETT÷BASExP))-IF(XD=1:CPN÷P:0))-(DURxP)
:(INV((YLD%÷P÷100+1))xDUR)-VOL+PRICE-PRIC
E)
```

(Ensure a space before/after OR above)

YLD%	CPN	P	SETT	BASE	MORE
CALL	XD	DUR	VOL	PRICE	MORE

For ex-div or at-issue calculations input 1 to [XD] (otherwise ensure that this value is always 0). The [PRICE] input is purely ornamental, for sharing purposes with the DIFF program below.

The values are shared with both the BONDS and DIFF programs BUT when using the BONDs program prior to employing the DURATION program the life input MUST be by the *days*, not the *dates*, method. Coming from the BONDS program all that is required is to press [DUR].

Example: Assume a price is 96.1875, a coupon of 5.5%, and a call 100. Assume, to, that the life and YTM have been calculated as 665 days and 7.777501%, respectively, (although it always best to find the precise [YLD%] on the BONDS program – see Appendix page 188).

YLD%	CPN	P	SETT	BASE	MORE
7.777501	5.5	2	665	365	

CALL	XD	DUR	VOL	PRICE	MORE
100	0	?	?	96.1875	

```
DURATION = 1.741121   VOLATILITY = 1.675947
```

```
[RCL] YLD% [÷] 200 [+] 1 [=] [STO 3]      = 1.038888
[RCL] DUR  [÷] [RCL 3]    [=]             = 1.675947 VOLATILITY
```

Using the volatility method of calculation, what would be the new price if the YTM was raised by a *difference* of .16, namely a lift from 7.778 to 7.938%

Key in the following DIFF program:

DIFF:RND((1—VOL÷100xDIFF)xPRICE:FIX)=NEW

VOL	DIFF	PRICE	FIX	NEW

Ensuring that the *clean* price is correctly stated in [PRICE], continue with the last example above:

VOL	DIFF	PRICE	FIX	NEW
1.68	.16	96.1875	3	?

```
                           = 95.930 new price
```

If the difference is *less* than the existing YTM treat the value as a *negative:*

```
 VOL     DIFF   PRICE    FIX    NEW
1.67    -.16   96.1875   3      ?   = 96.445 new price
```

The calculations are below:

```
Price   - ((price  x volatility/100   x difference) = new price
96.1875 - (96.1875 x   1.675947/100)        .16      = 95.929572
96.1875 - (96.1875 x   1.675947/100  x     -.16   ) = 96.445428
```

By keystrokes:

```
1 [-] [(] [RCL]  VOL  [÷] 100 [x] .16 [=] [x] [RCL] PRICE = 95.929572
1 [-] [(] [RCL]  VOL  [÷] 100 [x]-.16 [=] [x] [RCL] PRICE = 96.445428
```

Such calculated prices are not precise, but can be considered accurate to 2 places of decimals. Employing the BONDS program the new yield of 7.777501 + .16, namely 7.937501%, will find a clean price of 95.927405.

Example: Assume a 6% bond, semi-annual, ex-div, with a YTM of 15% and a call of 100. The days between settlement and maturity are 4019 with 4 a/i days. Find the duration and volatility. As the price is not provided, and as the structure of the duration program needs the price, it is necessary, first, to determine the clean price from the BONDS program:

```
[EXIT]  ↓↑ BONDS   CALC
 YLD%    PRICE    SETT     MAT     A/DTE    MORE
  15       ?      4019                -4
 BASE     CPN      P       CALL      XD      MORE
 365       6       2       100        1
 SINT                                        PRICE   = 52.205681
   0


[EXIT]   ↓↑ DURATION  CALC
 YLD%    CPN       P      SETT    BASE    MORE

 CALL     XD      DUR     VOL    PRICE    MORE
          ?        ?
DURATION = 6.956580  VOLATILITY = 6.471237
```

CHAPTER 10

The UK Market and Anomaly Bonds

The UK Market

In the UK market, unlike the US or Euro markets, there are no rules as to how bond yields are to be calculated, although there are a few conventions; such as that the base will be the actual calendar (365), the interest payments will be semi-annual and the quotations will be clean prices (a comparatively recent innovation!). Some of the comments and calculations relating to the UK market that follow may be useful, in general terms, to other markets.

Redemption Dates. When a bond is listed with two dates for redemption, take the longest date if the clean price stands below par (100). The converse is also true.

Settlement. For government securities, and local government bonds, settlement is the day following purchase. But for industrial debentures (corporate bonds) settlement (which was previously linked to the London Stock Exchange fortnightly accounts system) is now 7 days after purchase as is the case in the Eurobond market.

Ex-dividends. With no system for bearer stocks, dividends for Government stocks are paid by the Bank of England to the registered holders of individual bonds. To avoid making payments to holders who have sold before the next due payment, and before re-registration could be effected, the Bank rules that all such securities shall be deemed to be ex-div some 37 days before the payment date. Consequently, an investor making a purchase between the X date and the next payment date will not receive any accrued interest due.

Example: A UK debenture with a coupon of 6%, a call of 100, a life of 4019 days, with four days to run to the next coupon date.

If the quoted ex-div price is 54.50 what is the YTM%(XD)? If the days method is employed the a/i days will be input as a negative. The a/i is 4 [x] 6 [÷] 365 [=] [+/–] –0.065753

YLD%	PRICE	SETT	MAT	A/DTE	MORE
?	54.50	4019		−4	

BASE	CPN	P	CALL	XD	MORE
365	6	2	100	1	

SINT					
0	With 1 in SINT				

YLD% = 14.340214 compound
YLD% = 14.339416 simple

Sunday redemption. Some statisticians consider that if maturity falls on a Sunday the yield should be reduced fractionally to compensate for the fact that reinvestment, theoretically, cannot be immediate but must wait for the banks to open the following day.

$$(\text{YTM\% x days life}) \div (\text{days life} + 1) = \text{YTM\% (adjusted)}$$
$$10 \ \text{x} \ 665 \ \div \ 666 = 9.98\%$$

A UK problem – when settlement fringes a payment date
With computer or calculator programs, as opposed to normal mental agility, problems sometimes arise. One is as follows.

Assume a bond has a settlement date of November 14, 1988 and that maturity is November 15, 1991. In the UK such a bond is treated as an ex-div calculation for the purchase was obviously made one day prior to the next payment date, namely November 15.

It will be found that there are 1096 days-between and consequently there are some 6 (1096/182.5 = 6.005479) half annual periods and 1 day (.005479 x 182.5). If maturity was moved one half year earlier, namely May 15, 1991, surely one could confidently expect that there would be 5 periods and one day – and the new [n + k] would be 5.005479.

Unhappily, if dividing 912 (the number of days between settlement and the new advanced maturity date) by 182.5 the [n + k] factor becomes 4.997260. If this erroneous [n + k] factor is not recognised and is left unadjusted, the whole calculation will be inaccurate.

There are two remedies. The first is to switch to the HP bond program, A/A SEMI annual mode, as soon as this situation arises. The alternative is to retain the *incorrect* [n + k] factor but to treat the remaining calculation as being in cum-div mode, by entering 0 to the [XD] label and altering the negative value in [A/DTE] to positive. Obviously the *days* method must be used, not *dates*.

Taking the latter date above, a 10% coupon and a YTM of 12% what is the price?

First assume that the erroneous [n + k] factor had gone unnoticed, and is employed, and the ex-div accrued interest days are correctly input as a negative – the accrued interest being (1 x 10/365) equals –0.027397

YLD%	PRICE	SETT	MAT	A/DTE	MORE	
12	?	912		–1		

BASE	CPN	P	CALL	XD	MORE	SINT
365	10	2	100	1		0

The ex-div inaccurate price is found as 91.11

Now calculate in cum-div mode:

YLD%	PRICE	SETT	MAT	A/DTE	MORE	
12	?	912		1		

BASE	CPN	P	CALL	XD	MORE	SINT
365	10	2	100	0		0

Price = 95.78 (ex-div – by cum-div calc)

Out of interest, check with the HP in-built program for US Treasury bonds, namely the quasi-coupon method of calculation:

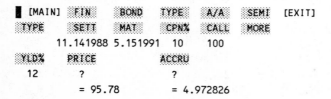

▌[MAIN]	FIN	BOND	TYPE	A/A	SEMI	[EXIT]
TYPE	SETT	MAT	CPN%	CALL	MORE
	11.141988	5.151991	10	100	

YLD%	PRICE		ACCRU
12	?		?
	= 95.78		= 4.972826

In this HP program the price is, of course, cum-div (hence the value of the accrued interest) for this method of calculation does not recognise ex-div requirements.

An alternative problem

This problem is the converse of the above; in that the bond is purchased one day *after* the last payment date. For example, a 12.50% bond with clean price of 102.125, a call of 100, with semi-annual payments, settlement March 15, 1988 and maturity September 14, 1997. Payment dates are 14th March/September.

The required days between settlement and maturity are 3,468 which, when divided by 182.5, finds an erroneous [n + k] factor of 19.002740. For in fact there are only 18 payment periods due between settlement and maturity and indeed this is confirmed if settlement was one day later (3,467/182.5 = 18.997260).

The remedy is to use the same methods as for the first kind of problem, but in reverse. Either switch to the US T Bond program as we did for the previous problem, which for this example will find a YTM of 12.12%, or treat this cum-div example as an ex-div calculation.

First, assume that the erroneous [n + k] factor has gone unnoticed and the cum-div accrued interest is correctly input as 1 x 12.5/365 = 0.034247

YLD%	PRICE	SETT	MAT	A/DTE	MORE	
?	102.125	3.151988	9.141997	3.141988		

BASE	CPN	P	CALL	XD	MORE	SINT
365	12.50	2	100	0		0

The cum-div incorrect [YLD%] is found as 13.27%

Now treat this requirement as an ex-div calculation by the input of 1 into [XD] and –1 into [A/DTE]. The YLD% will be found as 12.12% (cum-div – by ex-div calc)

The validity test

A computer program would need to ensure that such erroneous values do not go unnoticed. To test if settlement was *before* the next payment day, the first ex-div example, add .005 to the [n + k] value. If this changes the integer then action must be taken to adjust the calculation. Above 912 days between divided by 182.5 = 4.997260, and 4.997260 + .005 = 5.002260 – integer changed. Whereas the addition of .005 to one day more or less, namely (913/182.5) +.005 or (915/182.5) + .005 will be seen not to affect the integer.

For settlement *after* the previous payment date the solution will be the converse, namely the subtraction of .005. And taking the last example 3468 [÷] 182.5 [+] .005 changes the integer, whereas such a subtraction from days between of 3467 or 3469 will not affect the integers.

Both these two rather irritating and tiresome problems are, unhappily, not alleviated by finding, as some statisticians do, the exact number of odd days between settlement and the next payment date, as well as the precise number of payment periods between settlement and maturity. For in the last example the computer program would find, correctly, some 18 periods but would then be faced with 183 (March 15, 1988 – September 14, 1988) days being divided by 182.5, and the result added to the 18 periods provides the same erroneous [n + k] factor we had above!

Should the reader wish to consider the above on an annualised basis simply adjust, wherever necessary, by the factor 2. The verification factor of .005 above will, therefore, become .0025 with an annual base of 365.

Taxation requirements

A recent change in the UK market practice is that when calculating net yields, apart from the interest payments being treated as net of tax, the *accrued interest* will be also so treated. This has long been the custom in the USA. In practice, the accrued interest due *includes* the interest for any leap day intervening but it is optional whether this arrangement is used in calculating the yields.

Taking the cum-div 5.50% government bond example, with a clean price of 96.1875, a redemption value of 100, a term of 665 days, and a (gross) YTM% of 7.78%.   Find the net YTM% if the (income) tax rate is 25% net the coupon:

```
5.50 x .75    = 4.125    = net coupon    Press CPN
4.125 x 65/356 = 0.734589 = net accrued    96.1875 + .734589 = 96.9221
```

YLD%	PRICE	SETT	MAT	A/DTE	MORE	
?	96.1875	665		65		
	96.9221			0		

BASE	CPN	P	CALL	XD	MORE	SINT
365	4.123	2	100	0		0

```
                        YLD% = 6.37 Net YTM% and [÷].75
                             = 8.49% Grossed up Net
```

Assume that the above example now has a "small company" corporation tax requirement with tax at 25%. For calculation purposes the corporation tax, here, is equivalent to capital gains tax (CGT). Find the net YTM%. Adjust the [CALL] value:

```
100 - (100 - 96.1875 x.25) = 99.046875

Press    [RCL] CALL [=] [RCL] PRICE [=] 3.812500 [x]
.25 [-] [RCL] CALL [=] -99.046875 [+/-] press CALL
```

YLD%	PRICE	SETT	MAT	A/DTE	MORE	
?	96.1875	665		65		

BASE	CPN	P	CALL	XD	MORE	SINT
365	4.125	2	99.046875	0		0

```
                        YLD% = 5.85 Net YTM%
```

To find a price from a YTM% with a CGT content
Now we have a problem. Suppose that with a 25% overall tax rate for a small company you are asked to find the clean price from a net YTM of 8.44%, a gross coupon of 10%, a call of 100 and a term of 665 days.

How can this be calculated when, to find the net redemption value, we subtract the price – and it is the price which we are trying to find? Some statisticians avoid the isssue by saying that such a requirement never arises!

Find a notional call to find a notional price
If the tax rate was 25% the notional RV would be 100 – 25 =
75. But should the call be any value other than par (100) this
simple subtraction will not obtain. For if the call was 102 the
notional RV would *not* be 77, but 76.50!

This is found from:

Call x (1 – (tax rate%/100)) = 102 x (1 – 25/100) = 76.50 RV^n

Assuming a semi-annually paid nominal *net* coupon of 7.70%,
a life of 665 days, an accrued interest of 7.50 x 65/365 =
1.335616 and a yield to maturity, [YLD%], of 8.55% Find the
price if the capital gains tax, or corporation tax, was 25%.
Input the values known and a notional call of 75:

YLD%	PRICE	SETT	MAT	A/DTE	MORE	
8.44	?	665		65		
BASE	CPN	P	CALL	XD	MORE	SINT
365	7.500	2	**75**	0		0

PRICE = 76.920529 notional *clean* price
[STO 0]

The notional price *must* be a price *clean* of the net a/i.

The trick, now, is to find a method which will convert the
notional clean price (in this example of 76.92) to a true clean
price. The formula is:

$$\frac{RV^t(1 + i/p)^{-n} + Da_{\overline{n}|} + D}{(1 + i/p)^k} = NP\ (DP) - a/i = NP\ (CP)\ldots\ldots$$

$$\text{divided by}\quad 1 - \frac{CGT/100}{(1 + i/p)^{n+k}} = CP$$

Notional price	÷ (1 – ((CGT/100) x (1 + i/p)^–n + k))	=	Price
[RCL 0]	÷ (– (.25 x 1.042200^–665/182.5)) =		"
76.920529	÷ (1 – (.25 x 0.860180)	=	"
"	÷ (1 – .215045)	=	"
76.920529	÷ 0.789553		97.993548

Check: Now knowing the net price, from a given net YTM, a check must be made to see if it is correct.

100 − (.25 x (100 − 97.993548)) =   press CALL

YLD%	PRICE	SETT	MAT	A/DTE	MORE	
8.44	?	665		65		

BASE	CPN	P	CALL	XD	MORE	SINT
365	7.50	2	99.498387	0		0

PRICE = 97.993548

Q.E.D.

(See Appendix page 190 for further related formulae)

When the first coupon differs from the remaining payments
Sometimes the first payment after an issue differs from the remaining payments. For example, assume a 13.25% UK government issue at 100.00 on July 17, 1975 to be redeemed (at par) on July 22, 1997. The half annual payment dates conventionally being 22 Jan/July, it would be absurd for interest to be paid on 22 July only five days after issue; so, sensibly, the Bank of England stated that it would pay an increased payment on the first payment date January 22, 1976 – some 189 days after issue.   13.25/2 x 189/182.5 = 6.860959, rounded up to 6.87 (the lender's benefit).

Once the first normal "anniversary" payment date (Jan 22, 1976) is passed all calculations become conventional, but if settlement occurs between issue date and the first payment date, the interest payment is 6.87 – instead of 13.25/2.

Look back at the listing of the BONDS program: now alter your existing program by deleting the wide spaced **CPN ÷ P** and type in **PMT** instead.

Being at issue there is no accrued interest but it is not necessary to go into XD mode, for there is a k factor. The life is 7959 days *less one period*, so ((7959/182.5) − 1) x 182.5 = 7776.5 days. Input to [SETT]. If the price is 96 find the YTM%:

YLD%	PRICE	SETT	MAT	A/DTE	MORE		
?	96	7776.5		0			

BASE	CPN	P	CALL	PMT	MORE	XD	SINT
365	13.25	2	100	6.87	YLD% = 14.268306		

Alternatively, take a 9.50% UK government issue January 14, 1976 at 93.25 to be redeemed at 100 on May 14, 1980, the payment dates being 14 May/November. The Bank of England stated that the first interest payment due on May 14, 1976, instead of 4.75, would be 9.50/2 x 120/182.5 = 3.123288, rounded to 3.13 There are 1580 days between issue and maturity. Find the YTM% at issue.

■ [CLEAR DATA]

YLD%	PRICE	SETT	MAT	A/DTE	MORE		
?	93.25	1580		0			
BASE	CPN	P	CALL	PMT	MORE	XD	SINT
365	9.50	2	100	3.13	YLD% = 11.535 at issue		

Do not forget to reconstitute the your BONDS program.
To undo PMT key in CPN ÷ P

When the call date is not the coupon date anniversary It is rare for a public bond issue to have the redemption date and the final date of the interest payment not matching. For an awkward issue date, as seen above, is usually overcome by adjusting the first payment, or the date on which it is made.

But there are some occasions when difficulties do occur, for example loan issues that are not on offer to the general public but are private contractual arrangements between, say, institutions and local government authorities. The reason why difficulties can occur with such bonds is that even today local authorities are somewhat inflexible with regard to their interest payment dates. The long established custom in many authorities is that interest payments will be made only twice a year, usually on March 31 and September 30.

While such bonds are rarely bought and sold it is often necessary, for valuation purposes, to be able to determine the price at any point in time between the original issue date and the final redemption date. And so it is necessary to know how to calculate prices and yields when the last interest payment is before or after the final redemption repayment.

Maturity after last payment date (LPD)

Assume a 2.50% LGA bond issued July 27, 1985 for three years, the final redemption date being July 27, 1988. Redemption value, [CALL], is 100 and the issue price is 83.47. This as we shall see later provides an YTM% at issue of 9.25% The dates for payment by this LGA are March 31 and September 30.

The first thing to remember in this type of calculation is that the date of redemption is not important; what is important is the last payment date, from which interest is added or subtracted. The life of the above example, therefore, is not July, 27 1985 through to July, 27 1988 but is July, 27 1985 to March 31, 1988, namely 977 days (naturally ignoring any leap days). And the number of interest days from last payment date (3.311988) to final maturity (7.271988) is 118 days.

First, the price, assuming no anomolies:

▌ [MAIN]   SOLVE   ↓↑   BONDS   CALC

Normally 1 should be input to [XD] for an at issue calculation but not here because the structure of the bond provides some odd days, namely 977/182.5 = 5.353425. Being at issue there is, naturally, no a/i, so input 0 into [A/DTE].

YLD%	PRICE	SETT	MAT	A/DTE	MORE	
9.25	?	977		0		

BASE	CPN	P	CALL	XD	MORE	SINT
365	2.50	2	100	0		0

PRICE = 85.114317 at issue

Now find the correct interest due for the odd 118 days between the last interest payment date and the final redemption date. Payments must always be rounded:

```
2.5/2   x 118/182.5 = 0.80219                =   .81
Add this to the call, 100 + .81             = 100.81
Discount this value from final maturity date
100.81 ÷ (1 + 9.25/200)^(118/182.5)         =  97.905661
```

Assuming that the above values are still *in situ*, with 97.905661 on display press [CALL] and then repress [PRICE] = 83.470210

This is how a "one-off" is calculated; should the requirement be a continuing one, employ the program, which is semi-annually based, outlined below:

Key in the following **RV/BEFORE/AFTER/LPD** program:

```
RV/BEFORE/AFTER/LPD:SGN(YLD%)xPRICE=((SPP
V(YLD%÷2:INT(LIFE÷182.5)+ABS(ODDS)÷182.5)
x(100+RND((CPN÷2xODDS÷182.5):2))+CPN÷2)+(
USPV(YLD%÷2:INT(LIFE÷182.5))xCPN÷2))xSPPV
(YLD%÷2:FP(LIFE÷182.5))
```

| YLD% | PRICE | LIFE | ODDS | CPN |

The program assumes semi-annual payments, a half year as 182.5 days, and values at a dirty price. The prices at issue are of course clean of a/i.

▌ [MAIN]

SOLVE	↓↑ RV/BEFORE/AFTER/LPD		CALC	
YLD%	PRICE	LIFE	ODDS	CPN
9.25	?	977	118	2.50

= 83.470210

If a valuation was to run from August 1, 1986 the life would be 607 days with, as before, 118 days to run to maturity.

YLD%	PRICE	LIFE	ODDS	CPN
	?	607		

= 88.85

Since the yield is assumed for the purposes of valuation, the price found is usually the dirty price, the additional accrued interest being considered irrelevant. But if a clean price is required for other reasons, find the correct number of calendar days from settlement or valuation day back to the last payment date: in the above example it would be 5 days, (5 x 2.5/2) ÷ 182.5 = 0.034247 and 88.85 − .034247 = 88.81. In these circumstances the (1 − k) method must never be used.

The actuarial formula where maturity is after LPD:

$$\frac{(RV + (D \times t)) \times (1 + i/p)^{-n+t} + Da_{\overline{n}|} + D}{(1 + i/p)^{k}} = Price + a/i$$

(The interest (D x t) above must always be rounded to £/p before being added to the [RV], for this is a cash receipt)

Maturity before Last Payment Date (LPD)
This structure is a somewhat rare occurrence: a 9% bond with a YTM of 15%, with a life (valuation date – LPD) of 725 days with 118 days interest *not liable*, the final payment being the redemption value plus coupon *less* the 118 days interest.

The program, provided above, can be employed, save that the odd days, [ODDS], are input as a *negative*.

YLD%	PRICE	LIFE	ODDS	CPN
15	?	725	–118	9
	= 84.62			

For the converse, when maturity is *before* the LPD, the RV + (D x t) converts to RV – (D x t) in the above formula.

Split coupons – convertibles
Sometimes bonds are issued with different coupon values for different periods within the full term of the loan.

Assume an issue price of 90, an RV of 100 over a term of 20½ years. Interest is paid semi-annually, 8% nominal for 4½ years and 12% nominal for the remaining 16 years. What is the YTM% at issue?

The astute statistician will immediately appreciate that, because the bond is "at issue", having no odd days, this problem can easily be solved by finding the IRR:

▌ [MAIN] FIN CFLO ▌ [CLEAR DATA] YES

```
90  [+/−] = −90    [INPUT]
 8  [÷] 2 =   4    [INPUT]   4.5 [x] 2 [=]          9  [INPUT]
12  [÷] 2 =   6    [INPUT]   16  [x] 2 [−] 1 [=] 31   [INPUT]
            106    [INPUT]                            [INPUT]
```

[EXIT] CALC IRR% = 5.760043
and [x] 2 [=] 11.520% YTM AT ISSUE

To find the gross (flat) yield needs a little thought. Normally the flat yield is (coupon x 100/price) but in this case, with two coupons, the final value used must be the result of a weighted mean calculation.

$$\frac{(cpn \times per) + (cpn \times per)}{per + per} = \frac{(8 \times 4.5) + (12 \times 16)}{4.5 + 16} = 11.12\% \text{ COUPON}$$

and 11.121951 x 100/90 = gross (flat) yield = 12.36%

This particular calculation is outlined in Chapter 8, using either the HP weighted mean program facilities or the W/MEAN program supplied, which is useful for short WM requirements.

The actuarial formula for split coupons is:

$$\frac{RV(1 + i/p)^{-n} + Da_{\overline{n}|} - (D - D')a_{\overline{n'}|} + D'}{(1 + i/p)^{k}} = DP$$

Where D'= the first [CPN1], D = the second [CPN2], and n' = first CPN period, shown in the program as [FIRST].

Taking the above example, with the YTM% as 11.520086% at issue:

$$\frac{100(1.0576^{-41}) + 6a_{\overline{41}|} - (6-4)\,a_{\overline{9}|} + 0.00}{1.0576^{0.00}} = 90.00 \quad \text{issue CP}$$

(the 0.00 factors stand above because the bond was "at issue")

Key in the following **SPLIT/CPNS** program:

```
SPLIT/CPNS:SGN(YLD%)xPRICE+ACCRU=(XD-XD)+
SGN(N)x((SPPV(YLD%÷2:INT(N))xCALL)+(CPN1÷
2)-IF(XD=1:(CPN1÷2):0)+SGN(FIRST)x((USPV(
YLD%÷2:INT(N))xCPN2÷2))-(USPV(YLD%÷2:FIRS
T)x(CPN2÷2-CPN1÷2)))xSPPV(YLD%÷2:FP(N))
```

YLD%	PRICE	ACCRU	XD	N	MORE
CALL	CPN1	FIRST	CPN2		MORE

The program assumes semi–annual interest payments, [YLD%] and [CPN] have nominal format. [FIRST] = the number of payment periods for first coupon.

Filling in the data from the at issue example above:

YLD%	PRICE	ACCRU	XD	N	MORE
?	90	0	**1**	41	

CALL	CPN1	FIRST	CPN2
100	8	9	12

YLD% = 11.52

Assume that settlement occurred leaving a life of 6662 days, the number of payment *periods* (ignoring odd days) for the first coupon is $41 - (6662/182.5) = 4 \ldots$

YLD%	PRICE	ACCRU	XD	N	MORE
?	90	0	0	6662/182.5	

CALL	CPN1	FIRST	CPN2
100	8	4	12

YLD% = 12.61% working to a dirty price of 90.

Working to a clean price of 90, and assuming 91 accrued interest days, input (91x4/182.5) = 1.994521 into [ACCRU] and repressing [YLD%] = 12.32%   Alternatively, leaving 12.61 in [YLD%] unaltered but re-pressing [PRICE], the clean price becomes 88.01.

Convertibles
This split coupon program can be employed for convertibles, for in effect such bonds have two coupons.

For example, a 9% bond, semi-annual interest paid, was issued at 100 with 100 to be paid at redemption in March 1980.   It is converted into a 9% stock to be redeemed at 110 in March 2000.   Every unit of £100 held before conversion would be worth £110 after conversion.

As a result, the 9% coupon is now worth 9.90% and, in the same way, the 100 RV will be worth 110.   If an investor purchased stock 1412 days *prior* to conversion at 94.75 (CP), what was his YTM% at purchase?

The [N] value must be (20 x 2) + (1412/182.5) = 47.736986 and the [FIRST] becomes just the periods (47 – 40) = 7. The first coupon, [CPN1] = 9, the second coupon, [CPN2], 9.9 and the accrued interest becomes:

$$(1 - FRAC(1412/182.5)) \times 9/2 = 1.183562$$

YLD%	PRICE	ACCRU	XD	N	MORE
?	94.75	1.1836	0	47.737	

CALL	CPN1	FIRST	CPN2		
110	9	7	9.9	YLD% = 10.276 YTM%	

Annuity bonds
Annuities, like mortgages, are calculated so that all capital and interest repayments are made during the life of the bond, consequently there is no redemption amount due to the investor at maturity. At the time of writing there are no such bonds traded on the UK bond market, but there have been in the past and there is no reason why there should not be others in the future.

Perhaps the best way to understand annuity bond calculations, which are obviously substantially different from conventional methods, is to take the example of one such bond which came to maturity at the end of 1988.

On October 15, 1980 Zimbabwe made an issue of an annuity bond with a nominal annual interest rate of 10.25%, with payments of £50 each half year. The payments were in arrears, consequently the first interest payment was on April 15, 1981. The final payment would be on October 15, 1988.

These payments provide a present value (loan amount) of:

$$50a_{\overline{16}|} \text{ at } (10.25/2)\% = PV$$

$$50 \times ((1- 1.05125^{-16})/.05125)) = £537.10 \text{ rounded.}$$

Remember in this type of bond there is no redemption value or call, for once the bond has matured all the repayments have been completed and there is nothing more to come.

The dirty price/YTM are simple to calculate in that the equation is the same as that for any normal bond yield calculation – save that there is no call value.

If, therefore, settlement occurred on February 23, 1984 it will be found that there are 1694 days to maturity (October 15, 1988), ignoring any leap days intervening.

Dividing this days-between factor by 182.5 we obtain an [n+k] of 9.282192 and, assuming a YTM of 13%, the dirty price can be found by employing the BONDS program:

[MAIN]	SOLVE	↓↑	BONDS	CALC			
YLD%	PRICE		SETT	MAT	A/DTE	MORE	
13	?		1694		0		
BASE	CPN		P	CALL	XD	MORE	SINT
365	100		2	**0.00**	0		0

(retain values input)

PRICE = 376.062479 DP
dirty

The clean price

Nowadays, with clean price quotations, difficulties arise! To find the accrued interest first examine a schedule of the loan.

The issue date is October 15, 1980 and present value = £537.10

#	DATE	BAL	RATE/200	INTEREST	PMTS	End Month Balance
1	15 April 81	537.10 x	.05125	= 27.53 + 537.10 − 50		= 514.63
2	15 Oct 81	514.63 x	"	= 26.37 + 514.63 − 50		= 491.00
3	15 April 82	491.00 x	"	= 25.16 + 491.00 − 50		= 466.16
4	15 Oct 82	466.16 x	"	= 23.89 + 466.16 − 50		= 440.05
5	15 April 83	440.05 x	"	= 22.55 + 440.05 − 50		= 412.60
6	15 Oct 83	412.60 x	"	= 21.15 + 412.60 − 50		= 383.75
7	15 April 84	383.75 x	"	= 19.67 + 383.75 − 50		= 353.42
8	15 Oct 84	353.42 x	"	= 18.11 + 353.42 − 50		= 321.53
9	15 April 85	321.53 x	"	= 16.48 + 321.53 − 50		= 288.01
10	15 Oct 85	288.01 x	"	= 14.76 + 288.01 − 50		= 252.77
11	15 April 86	252.77 x	"	= 12.95 + 252.77 − 50		= 215.72
12	15 Oct 86	215.72 x	"	= 11.06 + 215.72 − 50		= 176.78
13	15 April 87	176.78 x	"	= 9.06 + 176.78 − 50		= 135.84
14	15 Oct 87	135.84 x	"	= 6.96 + 135.84 − 50		= 92.80
15	15 April 88	92.80 x	"	= 4.76 + 92.80 − 50		= 47.56
16	15 Oct 88	47.56 x	"	= 2.44 + 47.56 − 50		= 00.00

The accrued interest

The accrued interest in this type of loan is *not* the number of a/i days multiplied by the coupon and divided by 365; for since there is no final repayment of the loan at maturity, any interest due is repaid as part of the coupon – exactly like a mortgage, each payment containing both interest and capital.

The relevant period for interest must be determined before the interest due can be found. With settlement on February 23, 1984 it will be seen from the above schedule that the next following interest payment date is April 15, 1984 and the value of the interest due is £19.67.

It will be seen from the schedule that the interest period required, derived from the settlement date in question, is the seventh half year.

To find the interest rate employ the HP TVM discipline:

▌ [MAIN] FIN TVM OTHER 2 P/YR END [EXIT]
[DSP] FIX 2 [INPUT]
(this action is important, for the "fix" controls rounding of all
the [AMRT] calculations)

N	I%YR	PV	PMT	FV	OTHER
16	10.25	−537.10	?		

```
                         = 50.0000689546  reinput (rounded) 50 PMT
press OTHER   AMRT  6   #P  1  #P   displays #P PMTS: 7-7
press INT                          displays INTEREST=19.67
                                   (see schedule)
```

The notional accrued *days* can now be found by 19.67 x 131 (days between last payment date and settlement) ÷ 50 (the half annual interest = 51.535400. And so having recalled the BONDS program, employed just before the schedule was examined, with values still *in situ*, input 51.54 to [A/DTE]

▌ [MAIN] SOLVE ↓↑ BONDS CALC

YLD%	PRICE	SETT	MAT	A/DTE	MORE	
13	?	1694		51.54		
BASE	**CPN**	**P**	**CALL**	**XD**	**MORE**	**SINT**
365	100	2	0.00	0		0

```
                         PRICE = 361.941931
                         clean
```

In fact the actual accrued interest is found either from:
£19.67 (interest) x 131 (days) ÷ 182.5 (base) = £14.12
or
the dirty price (376.06) less the clean price (361.94) = 14.12

Ex-div calculations

There is no problem regarding ex-div calculations, for they are dealt with in the normal way, for ex-div calculations, on the BONDS program.

The Zimbabwe prospectus advised all annuitants that balances would be struck one month prior to the payment dates, in other words the stock would go ex-div on the 15th of March and September.

Assuming, with the same YTM of 13%, that if settlement occurred on April 2, 1984 (some 1656 days to maturity) the [n + k] factor would be 1656/182.5 = 9.073973 and the equation would become:

$$\frac{50 \times (1 - 1.065^{-9})/.065}{1.065^{.07397}} = 331.26$$

YLD%	PRICE	SETT	MAT	A/DTE	MORE	
13	?	1656		0		
BASE	CPN	P	CALL	XD	MORE	SINT
365	100	2	0	1		

PRICE = 331.26 (ex–div)
dirty

The accrued interest can be found either by calculation, below, or by subtracting the clean price from the dirty price.

`19.67 x 13/182.5 = 1.401151 accrued interest`

The interest (19.67), due on the April 15, 1984, multiplied by 13 (the a/i days), and divided by 50 = 5.114200, so input 5.11, *as a negative*, to [A/DTE]:

YLD%	PRICE	SETT	MAT	A/DTE	MORE	
13	?	1656		−5.11		
BASE	CPN	P	CALL	XD	MORE	SINT
365	100	2	0	1		

PRICE = 332.658472
clean

`The dirty price (331.26) − clean price (332.66) = −1.40 ex-div.`

Annuity capital and payments

So far it has been assumed that the annuitant holds £100 annuity (£50 each half year) represented by the annuity capital amount of £537.10 Consequently an annuitant capital of (say) £98.01 will entitle the accepting holder to an annuity of £18.25 (£9.13 each half year).

```
            £98.01 x 100/537.10 = £18.25  annuity
Or, alternatively: £55.78 x 537.10/100 = £299.59 capital value
```

Net calculations

The conventional method of netting the coupon cannot be employed for this type of bond nor, regrettably, can the MIRAS method of netting the issued interest rate to find a net payment basis. In fact there is, unhappily, no short cut by employing a conventional formula and so a specific formula, with a series of complex calculations, is required.

As annuity bonds are a rather rare trade it is not proposed to outline all the ramifications of a net presence here but a program can be supplied if required.

Should any reader wish to delve more deeply into annuity bonds, *Financial Calculations for Business* (also published by Kogan Page) covers fully the methods, formulae, schedules, calculations (including the complete net requirements), explanations, etc.

One final problem

An interesting point arose in the closing days of the Zimbabwe Government issue. With settlement on August 8, 1988 and some 68 days to run to maturity (October 15, 1988), one financial newspaper quoted a clean price of 47 ex-div, but no redemption yield.   And so to find the YTM, without thinking, I put the data into my BONDS program – to find a total blank!

For a moment I was somewhat nonplussed, until I realised that with annuity bonds, because all the debt is fully repaid by the annuity periodic payments, once they have gone ex-dividend in the final period there is nothing more to come.

And, indeed, the conventional ex-div formula for bonds, with less than one period to run, well demonstrates this fact:

$$\frac{\text{Redemption Value}}{(1 + i/p)^\wedge k} \quad \text{or} \quad \frac{\text{Redemption Value}}{1 + (i/p \ \times \ k)} = \text{Ex-div Dirty Price}$$

and with no redemption value the answer is a lemon! That being so, how was it possible for the quote to be 47 as the ex-dividend clean price ?

In fact the press quotation was an error, in that the stock did not go ex-div until September 15, 1988 (see earlier comment on the prospectus) and consequently with 68 days to run to maturity the stock should have been quoted cum-div.

Earlier, the schedule on page 160 (or calculating by AMRT as on page 161), shows the interest for period 16 is £2.44

With 68 days to run to maturity and a clean cum-div price of 47, as quoted, the YTM would be 16.25%, as instanced by the following simple interest calculation (not an unusual method with this short bond life).

As there are 183 days in the coupon period the (cum) accrued interest days, therefore, are 183 – 68 = 115 , which multiplied by the interest and divided by the coupon = 115 x 2.44/50 = 5.612; so input 5.61 to [A/DTE]:

[EXIT]	↓↑ BONDS		CALC			
YLD%	PRICE	SETT	MAT	A/DTE	MORE	
16.25	?	68		5.61		
BASE	CPN	P	CALL	XD	MORE	SINT
365	100	2	0	0		1

PRICE = 47.00
clean

With only 68 days to the end of the loan, and no maturity value, it was unlikely that there would be any trade in this particular stock. Consequently, it is probable that no one bothered to calculate the yield – and a price of 47 was a merely an educated guess as being somewhere near the final dividend (50), due in a few weeks time!

CHAPTER 11

Bills, Certificates of Deposit and Notes

Discounting bills

A bill of exchange is an order by one person requiring a
second person to pay a third. It is used as a method of
obtaining cash *now*, albeit a reduced amount, instead of
waiting for the original bill to fall due.   There are many
variations on this theme, ranging from the case of a small
business seller, who wants a lesser cash flow now rather that
waiting for his client to pay his bill in due course, to
governments borrowing short term, by means of the well
known Treasury or T bills.

A $1,000 bill due in 90 days time can be discounted in the
market for (say) 15%. This will provide a discount value of:

```
$1000 − (1000 x 15/100 x 90/360)  =  $962.50 discount value
$1000 − 962.50                    =  $ 37.50 discount amount
                          /365)   =  £963.01
                                  =  £ 36.99
```

The above example can be calculated by the HP in-built BUS
program:

```
▌ [MAIN]  BUS    %CHG
15 [x] 90 [÷] 365 [=] 3.698630 [+/.] and press  %CH
 OLD    NEW    %CH
1000     ?     -3.70
        = 963.01
```

On page 205 of the 17B *Owner's Manual* and page 253 of the
19B *Owner's Manual* there are two bill discounting programs,
based on the financial calendar (30/360).

The program provided below is suitable for calculating both
bill discounting and short term certificates of deposit.

Key in the following **BILLS/SHORT/CDS** program:

```
BILLS/SHORT/CDS:FACEx(RATE%xLIFE+BASEx100
)÷(BASEx100+SGN(PRICE)xYTM%x(LIFE-C/DYS))
=PRICE
```

| FACE | RATE% | LIFE | BASE | PRICE | MORE |
| YTM% | C/DYS | | | | MORE |

The YTM% C/DYS labels relate to Short CD calculations only and should be ignored for bill discounting.

Taking the above example:

FACE	RATE%	LIFE	BASE	PRICE	MORE	YTM%	C/DYS
1000	−15	90	365	?		ignore	ignore

(note the negative)   = 963,01

FACE	RATE%	LIFE	BASE	PRICE	MORE
			360	?	

= 962.50 [−] 1000 = −37.50

The *banker's return* provides a somewhat different perspective. In the above example a banker lays out £963.01 (rounded please) in order to obtain £1,000, after a delay of 90 days. His return, therefore, must be:

```
1000 [÷] 963.01 [-] 1 [x] 365 [÷] 90 [x] 100 = 15.58% Yield
```

FACE	RATE%	LIFE	BASE	PRICE	MORE
963.01	?	(90)	365	1000	RATE% = 15.58

With the two HP programs mentioned above there is an example: "Price and Yield of a Discounted Note. What are the price and yield of the following US Treasury Bill: settlement date October 14, 1988; maturity date March 17, 1989; discount rate 8.7%?" (155 days between settlement and maturity).

FACE	RATE%	LIFE	BASE	PRICE	MORE
100	−8.7	154	360	?	

(note negative)   = 96.278333   RND to 96.28 press FACE

FACE	RATE%	LIFE	BASE	PRICE	MORE
96.28	?			100	RATE% = 9.03 Yield

In the States the financial calendar (30/360) is used as the base value but "actual" days are always taken for the term.

The answer given in the *Owner's Manual* is 9.04%, the reason being that the price was not rounded before being transported from the first HP program to the second HP program. In practice it is doubtful if the US Treasury provides a cash price of 96.278333 (recurring).

Discounting bills exceeding one year

Assume a bill has a face value of £1000 over a period of 500 days, with a lender's return required of 15%. The calculations to find the proceeds are as follows:

$$1{,}000.00 \div (1 + \frac{15 \times 365}{100 \times 365}) = 869.57$$

$$869.57 \div (1 + \frac{15 \times 135}{100 \times 365}) = 823.86$$

Using the above formula/program:

FACE	RATE%	LIFE	BASE	PRICE	MORE	YTM%	C/DYS	
?	15	365	365	1000		0	0	<-- ensure
= 869.57	[INPUT]	press	PRICE					

key-in 500 [-] 365 [=] 135 press LIFE

FACE	RATE%	LIFE	BASE	PRICE	MORE	YTM%	C/DYS
?		135		869.57			
= 823.86 proceeds							

If dollar discounting (30/360) is required change the [BASE] from 365 to 360.

If *semi*-annual discounting ("yankee dollars") exceeding one year is required, the precise number of days in each half year must first be determined, thereafter it is a straightforward calculation taking the half annual interest rate as the "working rate per cent".

Certificates of deposit

CDs can be bought and sold on the "secondary" market and the resulting immediate liquidity is an attraction to investors. CDs come in all shapes and sizes the world over, sterling and Eurodollar CDs being traded on the London market. "Yankee" dollars, as they are officially designated, are semi-annual CDs which are not traded in the UK – except by banks having US facilities.

Short-term certificates of deposit

$$\text{Principal} \times \frac{36,000 + (\text{interest rate\% x life in days})}{36,000 + (\text{yield rate\% x remaining days})} = \text{Price}$$

(for sterling calculations for 360 read 365)

Example: A Eurodollar CD of $50,000 (face value) issued with an interest rate of 16% (coupon) over a term of 90 days. The certificate is traded after holding for 60 days at a market rate (yield) of 15%. What is the price paid or the "proceeds"?

$$\$50,000 \times \frac{36,000 + (16 \times 90)}{36,000 + (15 \times (90-60))} = \$51,358.02$$

Using the above formula/program:

FACE	RATE%	LIFE	BASE	PRICE	MORE	YTM%	C/DYS
50000	16	90	360	?		15	60
				= $51,358.02			
			365	= £51,339.65			

Medium-term certificates of deposit

Finding the proceeds for medium-term CDs normally requires the making of a schedule; and schedules are best calculated on a computer rather than a calculator! Nevertheless the formula/program presented below can be employed, providing the user accepts interim working.

For example, a computer will find the proceeds of a medium term dollar CD with a face value of $50,000 with a coupon of 17%, traded at 16½%, with settlement August 19, 1982 and maturity June 15, 1985, as $51,887.19. For the program would take account of the fact that there would be an extra day in the second year (1984), which must be included in the schedule, and only 300 days in the last year.

A computer schedule would present as follows. It assumes that $50,000 x 17/100 x 365/360 = $8,618.06 interest for those years with the normal 365 days, whereas the interest in 1984 will be $8,618.06 x 366/365 = $8,641.67

$$\$(50,000.00 + 8,618.06) \;[\div]\; (1 + \frac{16.50 \times 365}{100 \times 360}) \;=\; \$50,217.15$$

$$\$(50,217.15 + 8,641.67) \;[\div]\; (1 + \frac{16.50 \times 366}{100 \times 360}) \;=\; \$50,403.61$$

$$\$(50,403.61 + 8,618.06) \;[\div]\; (1 + \frac{16.50 \times 300}{100 \times 360}) \;=\; \$51,887.19$$

proceeds

Key in the following **MEDIUM/CDs** program:

```
MEDIUM/CDS:PRICE=(VALUE+RND(FACExSGN(DAYS
)x(365+LEAP)xRATE%xSGN(YTM%)÷BASE÷100:2))
÷((YTM%x(DAYS+LEAP)÷BASE÷100)+1)
```

PRICE	VALUE	FACE	DAYS	LEAP	MORE
RATE%	YTM%	BASE			MORE

Taking the above example:

```
PRICE   VALUE   FACE    DAYS    LEAP    MORE    RATE%   YTM%    BASE
  ?     50000   50000   365     0               17      16.5    360
  = 50,217.15
```

```
Treat this price as the new VALUE  press [INPUT]
Press VALUE
```

```
PRICE   VALUE   FACE    DAYS    LEAP    MORE    RATE%   YTM%    BASE
  ?     50217.15                1   (see schedule - leap day)
  = 50,403.61
```

```
Again treat this price as the new VALUE  press [INPUT]  VALUE
PRICE   VALUE   FACE    DAYS    LEAP    MORE    RATE%   YTM%    BASE
  ?     50403.61        300     0   (see schedule - 300 days)
  = 51,887.19 = Proceeds ($)
```

Floating rate certificates of deposit (FRCDs)

In the examples given above, the value of the proceeds, the cost, was found from an interest rate which was "fixed", i.e. constant throughout the term.   But if this rate was changed (usually to a quarter of one percent above LIBOR, London Interbank Offered Rate) every six months, how would it be possible to find the cost?   The short answer is, not without some difficulty.

The formula used by the banks in Japan, where the floating rate method for CDs was dreamed up some years ago, is both long and cumbersome, in that a notional price is found from an assumed yield.   This price is then converted to "an equilibrium price", which is merely a price suitably rounded, up or down, according to taste!

The formula employed below is the author's somewhat shorter method, which is designed to provide a notional price so close to that found by the banking method that, after adjustment, the equilibrium quoted price will be the same.

Example: A floating rate CD (FRCD) of $500,000 has an investment rate of 17%. Settlement is on March 6, 1981, with maturity on May 5, 1983. To calculate a price for this type of certificate, the yield is always assumed. In this example it is assumed to be 10%.

$$(100 \times \frac{36000 + (cpn \times life\ days)}{36000 + (yield \times odd\ days)}) - \frac{cpn \times a/i\ days}{360} = notional\ price$$

There are 60 odd days [D/DYS] between settlement (3.061981) and the next payment   date (5.051981) with 121 accrued interest days [A/DYS] between settlement and the previous payment date (11.051980).

$$(100 \times \frac{36000 + (17 \times 181)}{36000 + (10 \times 60)}) - \frac{17 \times 121}{360} = 101.053871\ notional\ price$$

This notional price now has to be converted to an equilibium price, which will be either to 101 or, possibly, 101.0625, i.e. 101 & 1/16th.   The face value being $500,000 the quoted cost would be: $500,000 x 101.00/100 = $505,000.00

Sometimes there is a concession, to selected clients or for a substantial loan, and to scale down the price a "points spread" is   applied.   A "40 point spread" is .4% of the cost, here $500,000 x .004 = $2000 – a modest saving on half a million dollars!   ▸

Key in the following **FRCDS** program:

```
FRCDS:((36000+CPNx(A/DYS+O/DYS))÷(36000+Y
LD%xO/DYS)x100)-(CPNxA/DYS÷360)=N/PR
```

CPN	A/DYS	O/DYS	YLD%	N/PR		
17	121	60	10	?	= 101.053871	notional price

the remainder of the calculation is as above.

Forward rate agreements

Forward rates are reasonably simple to calculate. The interest from each nominal interest rate, based on number of days per period, is rolled up with the interest for the subsequent periods, and the total simple interest so engendered is treated as the *annualised* rate. Annualised, because in many cases the interest and periods will not be consistent with a full year.

The underlying reason for a program such as this is that although the annualised rate is often known, together with some of the period rates, it is the missing rates that are required.

The HP Business Calculators' programming format provides the ideal method of finding the infinite number of variables required.

Key in the following **FRA** program:

```
FRA:(AxBxCxDx0)+ANNU=365÷(D1+D2+D3+D4)x((
(AxD1÷36500+1)x(BxD2÷36500+1)x(CxD3÷36500
+1)x(DxD4÷36500+1))-1)x100
```

A	B	C	D	ANNU	MORE
D1	D2	D3	D4		MORE

Should HP's infra-red printer be employed, key in ANNUALISED instead of ANNU in order that the print out can reflect the full nomenclature.

The somewhat unorthodox first five values in the program have no mathematical merit, but have been inserted in order to format the menu; for it was found there was less likelihood of input error if the rates and periods were separated.

Assume the following FRA's: 8.875% for 92 days, 9.20% for 92 days, 9.07% for 91 days 9.32% for 90 days. What is the annualised rate%?

Data input can be in any order. As the days per period are likely to change less than the rates it may more convenient to input those values first.

D1	D2	D3	D4		
92	92	91	90	press	MORE

A	B	C	D	ANNU	MORE
8.875	9.20	9.07	9.32	? = 9.43%	

Any one of the above rates can be found, providing all the remaining required values are *in situ*. Assume an annualised rate of 10%, what is the rate for the last quarter?

A	B	C	D	ANNU	MORE
			?	10.00	

D1	D2	D3	D4		
				D = 11.47%	

Assume that there were only two relevant rates in the last half of a forward rate financial year, namely 8.75% for 91 days and 8.97% for the final 92 days. Find the annualised rate%.

▌ [CLEAR DATA]

A	B	C	D	ANNU	MORE
		8.75	8.57	? = 8.76%	

D1	D2	D3	D4		MORE
		91	92		

With the following FRA's what is annualised rate%:
9.31% for 92 days, 9.38% for 182 days and 9.46% for 91 days?

▌ [CLEAR DATA]

A	B	C	D	ANNU	MORE
9.31	9.38	9.46		? = 9.66%	

D1	D2	D3	D4		MORE
92	182	91			

Acknowledgements to Babcock & Brown, a London broking house, for advising the requirement and the method employed.

Hedged floating rate notes
A Eurodollar FRN is a negotiable interest-bearing security
with a coupon which is usually "fixed" at periodic intervals.

The calculation most usually required is to find the return
available when an investor buys a Eurodollar or a US-dollar
FRN and hedges into his own, or a required, currency.

Assume that a Deutschmark investor purchases a $1.0 million
FRN and the coupon is "fixed" at 11% (1/4 of 1% over 6
months LIBOR) on October 6, 1988. The coupon period runs
from October 6, 1987 – April 6, 1989, a period of 182 days.
The spot $/DM exchange rate is 2.50% and the (6 months)
forward $/DM exchange rate is 2.45% The price is 99.80

The investor hedges the same amount of dollars, which he
buys at the spot rate, over the next (refix) date, which in this
example is 182 days, as well as the dollar interest payment.

The calculations
The calculations are a good deal less complicated than they
might at first appear.

```
FRN x price/100                              = cost in $
    x spot rate                              = cost in DM
FRN x (price/100 + cpn x days/36000          = proceeds in $
    x forward rate                           = proceeds in DM

((DM proceeds/DM cost - 1) x 36000/days  = Yield% (annualised)
```

Key in the following program, **FRNS/HEDGE * ***

```
FRNS/HEDGE:IF(S(PRICE) OR S(PRCDS):FRNx(P
RICE÷100+(SGN(SPOT)xCPNxDAYS÷36000))xFWD-
PRCDS:((PRCDS÷(FRNxPRICExSPOT÷100))-1)x36
000÷DAYS-YLD%)
```

(Ensure a space before/after OR above)

```
FRN   PRICE   SPOT   CPN   DAYS   MORE
FWD   PRCDS   YLD%                MORE
```

This program finds the proceeds in the required currency (here DMs) and the yield%. Should the user require the cost, assuming the data has already been input:

```
[RCL] FRN [x] [RCL] PRICE [÷] 100 = COST IN $
           [x] [RCL] SPOT    = COST in required currency
```

Taking the above example, find the proceeds, yield% and cost in DMs

FRN	PRICE	SPOT	CPN	DAYS	MORE
1E6	99.80	2.50	11	182	

FWD	PRCDS	YLD%		MORE
2.45	?	?		

```
                               Proceeds = DM 2,581,347.22
                               Yield = 6.845559%
```

```
[RCL] FRN  [x]  [RCL] PRICE  [÷] 100 [=] $     988,000.00
           [x]  [RCL] SPOT            [=] DM 2,495,000.00
```

What would be the difference to the yield if the coupon period concerned included a leap day?

FRN	PRICE	SPOT	CPN	DAYS	MORE
				183	

FWD	PRCDS	YLD%	,	MORE
	?	?		

```
                               Proceeds = DM 2,582,095.83
                               Yield = 6.867177%
```

Notes with interest at maturity
Yet another type of interest bearing obligation is that of maturity discounting with rolled-up interest, namely a note with no coupon but with interest paid when the loan matures.

On page 115 of the Hewlett-Packard *Real Estate, Banking and Leasing* pamphlet two programs were provided and an example given for a US tax exempt note, a requirement which employs this type of calculation.

As such notes can be either 365 or 360 based, the pamphlet outlined two separate programs.

The example given, was for a note issued on January 4, 1988, to mature on July 5, 1988. Settlement was on March 21, 1988. The interest rate on the note was 5% and if the yield required is 6.2% what is the price?

The days between issue and settlement are 77 days, between issue and maturity 181 days, and between settlement and maturity 104 days. The calculations to find the price are:

```
((1 + (181/360 x 5/100)) ÷ (1 + (104/360 x 6.2/100)) x 100)
                    - (77/360 x 5) = 99.640415
```

Below is *one* program which covers both the 365 or 360 bases

Key in the following **NOTES/INT/MAT** program:

```
NOTES/INT/MAT:(DDAYS(ISSUE:SETT:SGN(MAT)x
IF(BASE=360:3:1)))÷BASExI%xSGN(YLD%)+PRIC
E=(1+(DDAYS(ISSUE:MAT:IF(BASE=360:3:1))÷B
ASE)xI%÷100)÷(1+(DDAYS(SETT:MAT:IF(BASE=3
60:3:1))÷BASE)xYLD%÷100)x100
```

ISSUE	SETT	MAT	BASE	I%	MORE
YLD%	PRICE				MORE

Taking the above example:

ISSUE	SETT	MAT	BASE	I%	MORE
1.041988	3.211988	7.051988	360	5	
YLD%	PRICE				MORE
6.2	? = 99.640615				

One further example: issue October 1, 1988, settlement March 17, 1989, maturity November 1, 1989. If the rate was 9½% and the price 100 1/16th what is the yield at maturity?

ISSUE	SETT	MAT	BASE	I%	MORE
10.011988	3.171989	11.011989	360	9.5	
YLD%	PRICE				MORE
?	100.0625				
= 8.999692					
= 9.00%					

APPENDIX I

Programs for the Business Calculators

INTRODUCTION

RND(VALUE:FIX)=RND

VALUE　FIX　RND

CHAPTER 1

FLAT/NOM/EFF:IF(S(FLAT%) OR S(TRUE%):((IN
V(FLAT%xYEARS÷100+1))xSGN(TRUE%)xYEARSxP)
—USPV(TRUE%÷P:YEARSxP):((SPFV(NOM%÷P:P)—1
)x100)—EFF%)

(Ensure a space before/after OR above)

FLAT%　YEARS　TRUE%　P　NOM%　EFF%

VULG/FRAC:IF(S(VALUE) OR S(VULG?):RND(FP(
VALUE)xBASE:0)—VULG?:VULG?÷BASE—FRAC)

(Ensure a space before/after OR above)

VALUE　BASE　VULG　FRAC

AGENTS:IF(S(CAT#) OR S(COM%):CAT#x20÷((LO
G(VALUE)—1)x2)—COM%:(VALUExCOM%÷100)—CASH)

(Ensure a space before/after OR above)

CAT#　VALUE　COM%　CASH

[PI]:SGN(TERM)x((USPV(YLD%:TERM)xSGN(COST)
xINCM)+(SOLDx(SPFV(YLD%:—TERM))))÷COST=[P
I]

TERM　YLD%　COST　INCM　SOLD　[PI]

CHAPTER 3

```
ODD/DAYS:(0xNxI%xPVxPMT)+IF(FP(N)=0:−PV−F
Vx(SPFV(I%:−N))):−PV−FVxSPFV(I%:−INT(N))+I
F(C=0:(−PVxI%÷100xFP(N)):−PVx(SPPV(I%:FP(
−N))−1)))÷IF(INT(N)=0:USPV(I%:N):USPV(I%:
INT(N)))=IF(INT(N)=0:0:PMTxIF(BEG=0:1:(1+
I%÷100)))
```

| N | I% | PV | PMT | FV | MORE |
| C | BEG | | | | MORE |

```
WRAP:(P-P)+LOAN−(PMTSxSGN(#PER)−(BAL−BAL)
)xSGN(P)x(USPV(YLD÷P:#PER))−BALx(SPPV(YLD
÷P:#PER))=WRAP−WPMTx(USPV(YLD÷P:WPER))−WB
ALx(SPPV(YLD÷P:WPER))
```

| P | LOAN | PMTS | #PER | BAL | MORE |
| YLD | WRAP | WPMT | WPER | WBAL | MORE |

CHAPTER 4

```
RULE78:IF(S(RBATE) OR S(CHRG):RND(((NxSGN
(CHRG)−MTH?)x(2x(N−MTH?+1)÷(Nx(N+1))xCHRG
)÷2):2)−RBATE:RND(((N−MTH?)xPMTS−RBATE):2
)−BAL)
```

(Ensure a space before/after OR above)

| N | CHRG | MTH? | RBATE | PMTS | BAL |

```
RULE78/INT:RND(INV(Nx(N+1)÷2÷CHRG)x(N−MTH
?+1):2)=INT
```

| N | CHRG | MTH? | INT |

```
CPP:IF(S(CPP) OR S(PMT):RND((SGN(LOAN)x(C
PP+I%÷100x(LOAN−(#PER−1)xCPP))):2)−PMT:RN
D((LOAN−#PERxCPP):2)−BAL)
```

(Ensure a space before/after OR above)

| LOAN | CPP | I% | #PER | PMT | BAL |

```
LOAN/INCR:IF(S(PV)    OR    S(PMTS):RND(PV÷(U
SPV(RATE%÷P:P)xUSFV((((INCR÷100+1)÷SPFV(R
ATE%÷P:P))-1)xSGN(ΣYRS)x100:#YR?)+((USPV(
RATE%÷P:ΣYRSxP-#YR?xP)x(1+INCR÷100)^#YR?)
÷SPFV(RATE%÷P:Px#YR?))):FIX)-PMTS:PVxSPFV
(RATE%÷P:PxΣYRS)-FV)
```
(Ensure a space before/after OR above)

PV	RATE%	P	INCR	ΣYRS	MORE
#YR?	FIX	PMTS	FV		MORE

```
LOAN/INCR/LIFT:SGN(#YR?)xRND((PMTSx(1+INC
R÷100)^(IF(#?>#YR?:INV(0):(#?-1)))):FIX)-
NEXT
```

#YR?	PMTS	INCR	#?	FIX	NEXT

CHAPTER 5

```
SAVINGS/INCR:IF(S(FV)    OR    S(PMTS):RND(FV÷(
USPV(RATE%÷P:P)x(RATE%÷P÷100+1)xSPFV(INCR
:ΣYRS)xUSFV(((RATE%÷P÷100+1)^P÷(INCR÷100+1
)-1)x100:ΣYRS)xSPFV(RATE%÷P:P)xSPPV(INCR:1
)):FIX)-PMTS:(FV÷(1+(RATE%÷P÷100))^(ΣYRSxP
)))-PV
```
(Ensure a space before/after OR above)

FV	RATE%	P	INCR	ΣYRS	MORE
FIX	PMTS	PV			MORE

```
SAVINGS/INCR/LIFT:SGN(ΣYRS)xRND(PMTSx((IN
CR÷100+1)^IF(#?>ΣYRS:INV(0):(#?-1))):FIX)
=NEXT
```

ΣYRS	PMTS	INCR	#?	FIX	NEXT

CHAPTER 6

```
BS/VALUES:IF(S(LOAN)    OR    S(PV):RND((LOANxN
OM%÷100xDAYS÷365)-(LOANxNOM%÷100xMTHS÷12)
-LOAN+FEES:2)-PV:RND(PV-((LOANxNOM%÷100xD
AYS÷365)-(PMTSxMTHS)+FEES):2)-LOS)
```
(Ensure a space before/after OR above)

LOAN	NOM%	DAYS	MTHS	FEES	MORE
PV	PMTS	LOS			MORE

BS/LAST:IF(S(FV OR S(PMTS):(0xNxNOM%xLOSx
PMTSxFV)+LOSxSPFV(NOM%:N)+USFV(NOM%:N)xPM
TSx12+FV:RND(FP(((INT(FV÷PMTS)+1)x(FVxNO
M%÷100)÷12)+FV)÷PMTSxPMTS:2)-LAST)

(Ensure a space before/after or above)

N	NOM%	LOS	PMTS	FV	LAST

BS/TAP:IF(S(NP) OR S(PMTS):(Nx12)+INT(INT
(((INT(FV÷PMTS)+1)x(FVxNOM%÷100)÷12+FV)÷P
MTS)+MTHS)-NP:RND((NPxPMTS)+LOAN+PV+LAST:
2)-TAP)

(Ensure a space before/after or above)

N	FV	PMTS	NOM%	MTHS	MORE
NP	LOAN	PV	LAST	TAP	MORE

MIRAS/CONSTANT:IF(S(XOVER) OR S(BASIC):(L
OAN-30000)÷USPV(I%:SGN(N)xSGN(BASIC)xXOVE
R)+(30000xI%÷100x(1-BASIC÷100))-(30000÷US
PV(I%x(1-BASIC÷100):N-XOVER)):RND((((LOAN
-30000)÷USPV(I%:XOVER)+(30000xI%÷100x(1-B
ASIC÷100)))÷12):FIX)-PMTS)

(Ensure a space before/after or above)

LOAN	I%	N	BASIC	XOVER	MORE
FIX	PMTS				MORE

CHAPTER 7

H.P.LOANS:IF(S(COST) OR S(PMTS):(COST-DEP
)x(1+(FLAT%÷100xSGN(P)x#PER÷P))÷#PER-PMTS
:(COST-DEP)÷PMTS-(USPV((((((EFF÷100)+1)^I
NV(P))-1)x100xP)÷P:#PER)))

(Ensure a space before/after OR above)

COST	DEP	FLAT%	P	#PER	MORE
PMTS	EFF				MORE

H.P.INSUR:PMTSx(COST-DEP)÷((COST-DEP)-(PM
TSx#PERxINS%÷100))=N/P

PMTS	COST	DEP	#PER	INS%	N/P

ANYSPREADRENT: $\left(-\left(\text{COST} + \text{COMM} \div \text{DEP}\right) - \text{BALL} \times \right.$
$\left(\text{SPPV}\left(I\%\,\text{YR} \div P\,\middle|\,\text{YR} : \text{PER}\right)\right)\right) \div$
$\left(\#\text{ADV} + \text{USPV}\left(I\%\,\text{YR} \div P\,\middle|\,\text{YR} : \right.\right.$
$\left.\left.\#\text{SPR}\right)\right) = \text{PMT}_S$

* SEE BACK
PAGE COVER

LEASING:((CAP-LIEU)-RESxSPPV(RATE%÷P:(#PE
R+IF(EXTRA=1:1:0))))÷IF(TYPE<>3:((USPV(RA
TE%÷P:#PER-#ADV))xIF(TYPE=1:((1+RATE%÷100
÷P))^-(#ADV-1):1))+IF(LIEU<>0:0:#ADV):((U
SPV(RATE%÷P:#PER))x(1+RATE%÷100÷P)+(#ADV-
1)))=PMTS

CAP	LIEU	RES	RATE%	P	MORE
#PER	EXTRA	TYPE	#ADV	PMTS	MORE

SKIP:IF(S(CAP) OR S(DUE):(((CAP-(RESxSPPV
(RATE%÷P:#PER)))x(SPFV(RATE%÷P:P)-1)))÷((
USFV(RATE%÷P:BEFORE)xSPFV(RATE%÷P:(P-BEFO
RE))+USFV(RATE%÷P:AFTER))x(1-SPPV(RATE%÷P
:#PER)))÷(1+RATE%÷P÷100)-DUE:DUEx(1+(RATE
%÷P÷100)-ORD))

(Ensure a space before/after OR above)

CAP	RES	RATE%	P	#PER	MORE
BEFOR	AFTER	DUE	ORD		MORE

CHAPTER 8
W/MEAN:IF(S(NEXT) OR S(Σ):((AxB)-ΣΣ)+NEX
T:(-B+Σ)-NXT)

(Ensure a space before/after OR)

A	B	ΣΣ	NEXT	Σ	NXT

MOV/AVE (adjustment to HP's moving average program):

LAST	MAVG	N

EXP/SMOOTH:[1ST]x.95+[2ND]x.05=NEXT

[1ST]	[2ND]	NEXT

MIRR:SGN(SAFE)xSGN(RISK)x(1+MIRR÷100)^Σ(L
:1:SIZEC(INV):1:#T(INV:L))=-Σ(J:0:SIZEC(I
NV):1:MAX(FLOW(INV:J):0)xUSFV(RISK:#T(INV
:J))xSPFV(RISK:Σ(L:J+1:SIZEC(INV):1:#T(IN
V:L))))÷(MIN(FLOW(INV:0):0)+Σ(J:1:SIZEC(I
NV):1:MIN(FLOW(INV:J):0)xUSPV(SAFE:#T(INV
:J))xSPPV(SAFE:Σ(L:1:J-1:1:#T(INV:L)))))

SAFE	RISK	MIRR

CHAPTER 9

```
JAP:YLD%xSGN(PRICE)xSGN(CPN)=SGN(N)x(CPN+
((CALL-PRICE)÷N))xCALL÷PRICE
```

YLD%	PRICE	CPN	N	CALL

```
BONDS:SGN(YLD%)xPRICE+0xSETT+0xMAT+IF(FP(
A/DTEx100)=0:A/DTE:DDAYS(A/DTE:SETT+0xMAT
:IF(BASE=360:3:1)))÷BASExCPN=IF(CPN<>0:+(
((SPPV(YLD%÷P:INT(IF(FP(SETTx100)=0:SETT:
DDAYS(SETT:MAT:IF(BASE=360:3:2)))÷BASExP)
))xCALL)+    CPN÷P    -IF(XD=1:CPN÷P:0)+CPN
÷PxUSPV(YLD%÷P:INT(IF(FP(SETTx100)=0:SETT
:DDAYS(SETT:MAT:IF(BASE=360:3:2)))÷BASExP
)))xIF(SINT=1:(1÷(1+YLD%÷P÷100xFP(IF(FP(S
ETTx100)=0:SETT:DDAYS(SETT:MAT:IF(BASE=36
0:3:2)))÷BASExP))):SPPV(YLD%÷P:FP(IF(FP(S
ETTx100)=0:SETT:DDAYS(SETT:MAT:IF(BASE=36
0:3:2)))÷BASExP))):CALLxSPPV(YLD%÷P:IF(FP
(SETTx100)=0:SETT:DDAYS(SETT:MAT:IF(BASE=
360:3:2)))÷BASExP))
```

YLD%	PRICE	SETT	MAT	A/DTE	MORE
BASE	CPN	P	CALL	XD	MORE
SINT					

DATES:DDAYS(DATE1:DATE2:IF(#?# = 1:1:IF(#?# = 2:2:IF(#?# = 3:3:3)))) = DAYS

DATE1	DATE2	#?#	DAYS

DURATION:IF(S(YLD%) OR S(DUR):SGN(YLD%)
xSGN(CPN)xSGN(P)x(((YLD%÷P÷100+1)^-INT(SE
TT÷BASExP))xCALLxSETT÷BASExP+(CPN÷P)÷(1-I
NV(YLD%÷P÷100+1))x((FP(SETT÷BASExP)-((YLD
%÷P÷100+1)^-(INT(SETT÷BASExP)+1))xSETT÷BA
SExP)+(1-(YLD%÷P÷100+1)^-(INT(SETT÷BASExP
)+1)x(YLD%÷P÷100+1))÷(1-INV(YLD%÷P÷100+1)
)x(INV(YLD%÷P÷100+1)))-IF(XD=1:((CPN÷PxFP
(SETT÷BASExP))):0))÷(((1÷(1-(1÷(YLD%÷P÷10
0+1))))xCPN÷P)x(1-(YLD%÷P÷100+1)^-(INT(SE
TT÷BASExP)+1))+(CALLx(1+(YLD%÷P÷100))^-IN
T(SETT÷BASExP))-IF(XD=1:CPN÷P:0))-(DURxP)
:(INV((YLD%÷P÷100+1))xDUR)-VOL+PRICE-PRIC
E)

(Ensure a space before/after OR above)

YLD%	CPN	P	SETT	BASE	MORE
CALL	XD	DUR	VOL	PRICE	MORE

DIFF:RND((1-VOL÷100xDIFF)xPRICE:FIX)=NEW

VOL	DIFF	PRICE	FIX	NEW

CHAPTER 10

RV/BEFORE/AFTER/LPD:SGN(YLD%)xPRICE=((SPP
V(YLD%÷2:INT(LIFE÷182.5)+ABS(ODDS)÷182.5)
x(100+RND((CPN÷2xODDS÷182.5):2))+CPN÷2)+(
USPV(YLD%÷2:INT(LIFE÷182.5))xCPN÷2))xSPPV
(YLD%÷2:FP(LIFE÷182.5))

YLD%	PRICE	LIFE	ODDS	CPN

SPLIT/CPNS:SGN(YLD%)xPRICE+ACCRU=(XD-XD)+
SGN(N)x((SPPV(YLD%÷2:INT(N))xCALL)+(CPN1÷
2)-IF(XD=1:(CPN1÷2):0)+SGN(FIRST)x((USPV(
YLD%÷2:INT(N))xCPN2÷2))-(USPV(YLD%÷2:FIRS
T)x(CPN2÷2-CPN1÷2)))xSPPV(YLD%÷2:FP(N))

YLD%	PRICE	ACCRU	XD	N	MORE
CALL	CPN1	FIRST	CPN2		MORE

CHAPTER 11

BILLS/SHORT/CDS:FACEx(RATE%xLIFE+BASEx100
)÷(BASEx100+SGN(PRICE)xYTM%x(LIFE-C/DYS))
=PRICE

| FACE | RATE% | LIFE | BASE | PRICE | MORE |
| YTM% | C/DYS | | | | MORE |

MEDIUM/CDS:PRICE=(VALUE+RND(FACExSGN(DAYS
)x(365+LEAP)xRATE%xSGN(YTM%)÷BASE÷100:2))
÷((YTM%x(DAYS+LEAP)÷BASE÷100)+1)

| PRICE | VALUE | FACE | DAYS | LEAP | MORE |
| RATE% | YTM% | BASE | | | MORE |

FRCDS:((36000+CPNx(A/DYS+O/DYS))÷(36000+Y
LD%xO/DYS)x100)-(CPNxA/DYS÷360)=N/PR

| CPN | A/DYS | O/DYS | YLD% | N/PR |

FRA:(AxBxCxDx0)+ANNU=365÷(D1+D2+D3+D4)x((
(AxD1÷36500+1)x(BxD2÷36500+1)x(CxD3÷36500
+1)x(DxD4÷36500+1))-1)x100

| A | B | C | D | ANNU | MORE |
| D1 | D2 | D3 | D4 | | MORE |

FRNS/HEDGE:IF(S(PRICE) OR S(PRCDS):FRNx(P
RICE÷100+(SGN(SPOT)xCPNxDAYS÷36000))xFWD-
PRCDS:((PRCDS÷(FRNxPRICExSPOT÷100))-1)x36
000÷DAYS-YLD%)

(Ensure a space before/after OR above)

| FRN | PRICE | SPOT | CPN | DAYS | MORE |
| FWD | PRCDS | YLD% | | | MORE |

NOTES/INT/MAT:(DDAYS(ISSUE:SETT:SGN(MAT)x
IF(BASE=360:3:1)))÷BASExI%xSGN(YLD%)+PRIC
E=(1+(DDAYS(ISSUE:MAT:IF(BASE=360:3:1))÷B
ASE)xI%÷100)÷(1+(DDAYS(SETT:MAT:IF(BASE=3
60:3:1))÷BASE)xYLD%÷100)x100

| ISSUE | SETT | MAT | BASE | I% | MORE |
| YLD% | PRICE | | | | MORE |

Penalties for early settlement
(according to the UK Consumer Credit Act regulations)

Early redemption is irritating to a lender in that it upsets his cash flow arrangements and often entails considerable paper work. Consequently he is entitled to demand a *penalty* to recover some of his cost. In the old days, the conventional penalty was "three months payments". Nowadays, the CCA rules that for early redemption of a loan under five years the rebate can be calculated as if it was *two* months ahead, namely two periods of interest can be added; if over five years then only one additional period is permissible.

Assume that a loan is for £5,000, over a term of 144 months, at a *flat* rate of 20% and that the borrower wishes to redeem the loan after only 11 months. If the lender imposes the maximum permissible penalty what is the final balance? As the CCA regulations assume that the Rule 78 method will apply, the calculations will be as a follows:

```
The "charge" is (144 x 118.06) - 5,000 = £12,000.64
The rounded payments per month will be:
(5,000 x 20/100 x 12 + 5000) ÷  144 = £118.06
```

As the redemption period is under five years, two periods of added interest are permissible as a penalty, so the "rebate" must be found for the (144 – 11 – **2**) = 131 periods

```
(131 x 132)/(144 x 145) x the "charge" = 9,938.46 rebate
Rebate - ((144 - 11) x pmts)        = 5,763.52 balance
```

Employ the PENALTY/RULE78 program outlined at the end of this section. This amended program is peculiar to the UK and should not be confused with the conventional Rule 78 calculations or program on page 39.

N	CHRG	MTH?	PNTY	RBATE	MORE
144	12000.64	11	2	? =	9,938.46

PMTS	BAL				MORE
118.06	? = 5,763.52 balance				

Assume the following payments were missed and made up in the first eleven months of the loan:

End of month 1.	118.06		End of month 7.	200.00
2.	118.06		8.	0.00
3.	30.00		9.	50.00
4.	0.00		10.	0.00
5.	75.00		11.	30.00
6.	118.06			

The simplest way to find the balance due at the end of the 11th month, taking account of the above series of payments, is by employing the [TVM] discipline.

First find the *true* rate of interest:

[MAIN]	FIN	TVM	OTHER	12 P/YR	END	[EXIT]
N	I%YR	PV	PMT	FV		
144	?	−5000	118.06	0		
	= 27.212463					

N	I%YR	PV	PMT	FV	
2	27.21	−5000.00	118.06	?	= 4,990.54

N	I%YR	PV	PMT	FV	
1	27.21	−4990.54	30	?	= 5,073.72

N	I%YR	PV	PMT	FV	
1	27.21	−5073.72	0	?	= 5,188.77

N	I%YR	PV	PMT	FV	
1	27.21	−5188.77	75	?	= 5,231.44

N	I%YR	PV	PMT	FV	
1	27.21	−5231.44	118.06	?	= 5,232.01

N	I%YR	PV	PMT	FV	
1	27.21	−5232.01	200	?	= 5,150.66

N	I%YR	PV	PMT	FV	
1	27.21	−5150.66	0	?	= 5,267.46

N	I%YR	PV	PMT	FV	
1	27.21	−5267.46	50	?	= 5,336.91

N	I%YR	PV	PMT	FV	
1	27.21	−5336.91	0	?	= 5,457.94

N	I%YR	PV	PMT	FV	
1	27.21	−5457.94	30	?	= 5,551.71

To find the value at the end of 11 months, if all the payments had been made in due time:

N	I%YR	PV	PMT	FV
11	27.21	–5000.00	118.06	? = 4,942.33

To find the interest due to missed and made-up payments £5,551.71 – 4,942.33 = £609.37

This interest due must be added to any calculation regarding the conventional balance, with or without penalties. In view of the default interest due, what would be the final balance if the lender decided that he not insist on a penalty:

▌[MAIN]	↓↑	PENALTY/RULE78	CALC		
N	CHRG	MTH?	PNTY	RBATE	MORE
144	12000.64	11	0	?	
				= 10,243.08	

PMTS	BAL				MORE
118.06	? = 5,458.90				

and, with interest due and no period penalty:

£5,458.90 + 609.37 = £6,068.27 balance due

Key in the following **PENALTY/RULE78** * *:

```
PENALTY/RULE78:IF(S(RBATE) OR S(CHRG):RND
(((NxSGN(CHRG)-MTH?-PNTY)x(2x(N-MTH?-PNTY
+1)÷(Nx(N+1))xCHRG)÷2):2)-RBATE:RND(((N-M
TH?)xPMTS-RBATE):2)-BAL)
```

(Ensure a space before/after OR above)

N	CHRG	MTH?	PNTY	RBATE	MORE
PMTS	BAL				MORE

Dates, Bonds, Duration and Diff:

The value of these four programs being interactive can be seen below – together with proof, if proof be needed, that the use of the volatility calculation results in values very near to the real thing.

To check the discrepancy between the actual rate and the rate found by the volatility method, take an example of a semi-annual 5½% bond, with a redemption value of 100, and a price of 96 3/16ths. Settlement is on January 1, 1989, with maturity being on October 28, 1990 (base 365).

Assume that the yield to maturity is increased by 1 percentage point, namely from 7.78% to 8.78%

As the DURATION program is to be used, and because we want shared values, the input method for the life of the bond, must be *days* instead of *dates*.

Using the four programs in order below:

DATES:

DATE1	DATE2	#?#	DAYS			
1.011989	10.281990	2	?	=	665	days
	10.281988		?	=	−65	a/i days

BONDS:

YLD%	PRICE	SETT	MAT	A/DTE	MORE
?	96.1875	665		65	

BASE	CPN	P	CALL	XD	MORE
365	5.5	2	100	0	

SINT					
0			YLD% = 7.777501 [STO 0}		

DURATION:

YLD%	CPN	P		SETT	BASE	MORE
CALL	XD	DUR		VOL	PRICE	MORE
		?		?		
		1.741121	1.675947			

DIFF:

VOL	DIFF	PRICE	FIX	NEW
	1		11	?

```
                     NEW = 94.575448373 [STO 0]
                         = 94.575
```

Revert to the BONDS program, and with the values *in situ*, find the true price:

```
[RCL YLD%] [STO 1] [+] 1 [=] 8.777501 [STO YLD%]
```

YLD%	PRICE	SETT	MAT	A/DTE	MORE
8.778	?	665		65	

BASE	CPN	P	CALL	XD	MORE
365	5.5	2	100	0	

SINT
0

```
              PRICE = 94.577   (true)
            [RCL 0] = 94.575   (per volatility)
              Diff: =    .002
```

Alternatively, by the input of the volatility calculated price find the related YTM:

```
[RCL YLD%] [STO 2] [RCL 0] = 94.575448 [STO PRICE]:
```

YLD%	PRICE	SETT	MAT	A/DTE	MORE
?	94.575448	665		65	

BASE	CPN	P	CALL	XD	MORE
365	5.5	2	100	0	

SINT
0

```
              YLD% = 8.77837281674
            [RCL 2] = 8.77750137986
```

The above demonstrates that, by increasing the YTM by one percentage point, the volatility method of finding the notional yield and prices are "nearly correct"

Taking a further example, a 6% bond, with a call of 100, and an *ex-div* price of 54.50. There are 4019 days between settlement and maturity and –4 accrued interest days (base 365).

If the yield to maturity was *reduced* by 1 percentage point, the reader, using the three inter active programs above, might care to find the inaccuracy between the true price and the volatility created price. 0.166 should be the difference found.

Further formulae for obtaining a price from net calculations, having a CGT content

On page 150 a formula was provided to convert a notional price into the true clean price when a net YTM is provided and it is required to find the price – when a capital gains feature is included in the tax requirements.

This formula only covers the conventional calculation: the other formulae differ, if the calculations relate to simple or compound interest discounting, and for the short short bonds (per <1) when the life of the bond is so short as not to have any further interest payments due.

(1) Per >1 compound interest discounting (as on page 150):

$$\frac{RV^t(1 + i/p)^{-n} + Da_{\overline{n}|} + D}{(1 + i/p)^k} = NP\,(DP) - a/i = NP\,(CP)\ldots\ldots$$

$$\text{divided by } 1 - \frac{CGT/100}{(1 + i/p)^{n+k}} = CP$$

(2) Per >1 simple interest discounting:

$$\frac{RV^t(1 + i/p)^{-n} + Da_{\overline{n}|} + D}{1 + (i/p \times k)} = NP\,(DP) - a/i = NP\,(CP)\ldots\ldots$$

$$\text{divided by } 1 - \frac{CGT/100}{(1 + i/p)^{n+k} \times (1 + (i/p \times k))} = CP$$

(3) Per <1 short short compound interest discounting:

$$\frac{RV^n + D}{(1 + i/p)^k} = NP \text{ divided by } 1 - \frac{CGT/100}{(1 + i/p)^k} = CP$$

(4) Per <1 short short simple interest discounting:

$$\frac{RV^n + D}{1 + (i/p \times k)} = NP \text{ divided by } 1 - \frac{CGT/100}{1 + (i/p \times k)} = CP$$

Short bond calculations

Before computers, sighs of relief could usually be heard when bonds with such a short time to run to maturity needed calculating! Since such bonds have no further payments before final redemption, there is no interpolation, no computer looping required, for the respective formulae present as follows:

The compound interest discounting formulae:

$$\frac{RV + D}{(1 + i/p)^k} = DP(CI)$$

$$100 \times p \times ((\frac{RV + D}{DP})^{1/k} - 1) = YTM\%(CI)$$

The simple interest discounting formulae:

$$\frac{RV + D}{1 + (i/p \times k)} = DP(SI)$$

$$100 \times p \times ((\frac{RV + D}{DP} - 1) \times 1/k) = YTM\%(SI)$$

With a clean price of 99 28/32nds (99.875) a 4.75% UK Government bond is settled on February 7, 1988. The bond is redeemed for 100 on May 15, some 98 later. What is the YTM?

The HP Bond program finds the yield as 5.164134%

If we put the data onto the BONDS program we get:

YLD%	PRICE	SETT	MAT	A/DTE	MORE
?	99.875	2.071988	5.151988	11.151987	

BASE	CPN	P	CALL	XD	MORE
365	4.75	2	100	0	

SINT					
0			YLD% = 5.275233		

The reason for this discrepancy is that the HP bond program treats the discounting of the odd days by simple interest and so if we input 1 into [SINT] we get 5.243054%

The HP program accepts the leap day, a total of 98 days, whereas the BONDS program ignores them and treats the "days between" as 97 days. Following the HP line then:

YLD%	PRICE	SETT	MAT	A/DTE	MORE
?	99.875	98		84	

BASE	CPN	P	CALL	XD	MORE
365	4.75	2	100	0	

SINT
1

YLD% = 5.189553

We are getting nearer! The HP bond program, as explained earlier, uses the number of days in the coupon period as the base, here (98+84) = 182 and so the n + k is 98/182. Incidentally, most UK statisticians would calculate by this method for this type of short bond.

To put this type of calculation onto the BONDS program merely requires a slight adjustment:

98/182 x 182.5 = 98.267231 and 84/182 x 182.5 = 84.230769
Remembering that the limitation is two decimal places, input 98.27 to [SETT] 84.23 to [A/DTE].

YLD%	PRICE	SETT	MAT	A/DTE	MORE
?	99.875	98.27		84.23	

BASE	CPN	P	CALL	XD	MORE
365	4.75	2	100	0	

SINT
1

YLD% = 5.164131

c.f. the above HP YLD% = 5.164134

The fractional difference to the 6th place of decimals stems from the imprecise entry, due to the decimal limitation. Reverting to the SI formula above:

The DP = 99.875 + (2.375 x 84/182) = 100.971154

(((100.00 + 2.375)/100.971154) − 1) x 182/98 x 200 = 5.164134 YTM%

More about the ODD/DAYS program
(The cost of ignoring invoice discounts)

Readers may recall that on page 26 it was stated that the ODD/DAYS program was designed to equate, as near as possible in format, to the "top line of keys" of the old HP-12C Financial Calculator and to perform the same calculations.

Consequently, it will be appreciated that the algorithm, for both the HP-12C and the ODD/DAYS program, assumes that the fractional part of the [N] label relates to the odd days for any calculation rather than the method used by the [TVM] discipline.

The HP-12C usage had one limitation, namely that when [N] was pressed, the resulting value was only an integer.

Although this was understandable, for to obtain the number of odd days is a complex calculation, none the less, it was often extremely irritating.

With the user's help, the ODD/DAYS program has overcome this limitation.

Examples:
In many countries a cash discount is given to a purchaser providing he or she pays within a specified time. In the States, for example. a conventional method is to allow a 2% discount if the bill is paid within 10 days, if not it must be paid within 30 days, denoted on the invoice as "2/10, NET 30".

If the discount offer is ignored the loss is not, as some may think, merely 2%, but is, in fact, a good deal more.

In the HP *Business Finance and Accounting* solutions pamphlet (for the HP17B, 19B and 27S), page 29, examples and a program are provided. A special program, however, is not necessary, for the same results can be obtained by using the ODD/DAYS program, outlined in Chapter 3.

For instance, taking the above example (2/10, NET 30), what is the cost, in terms of annual interest lost, if the offer is not taken up? The calculation, employing either the 365 or 360 calendar, is as follows:

$$\frac{\text{the discount\% x 100 x the calendar days}}{(100 - \text{the discount\%}) \times (\text{total days} - \text{discount days})} = \text{cost\%}$$

$$\frac{2 \times 100 \times 360}{(100 - 2) \times (30 - 10)} = 36.73\%$$

Applying the ODD/DAYS program to this examples:

N	I%	PV	PMT	FV	MORE
20/360	?	−98	0	100	
	= 36.734694				

C	BEG				MORE
0	0				

To find the number of discount days, start from scratch with 0 [STO N]. Assuming that [I%] holds the full value found above, press [N]. The result will be a series of [LEFT] and [RIGHT] values on display. Press [CLR] and [N = 1] will display.

To assist the program guess a possible value and then press [N] [INPUT] [N] [N].

In this case try a value less than 1, namely .5 [N] [INPUT] [N] [N] = 0.0555556 will display: and x 360 = 20 discount days.

The above calculation employed only [PV] and [FV]. Refer to page 26 for an example with payments:

N	I%	PV	PMT	FV
?	.906716	−3500	115.01	0

C	BEG			MORE
0	0			

▌[CLEAR DATA] and input all the values *except* 36.6 to [N].

To find the correct [N] value of 36.60, namely 36 months and (0.6 x 360 ÷ 12) 18 odd days, 0 press [N] [N]. The [LEFT] and [RIGHT] values display, with [N = 1] after pressing [CLR].

Now make a guess and continue iterating until the display for [N] is an *integer.*

This time, guess a value greater than 1: try 50 [N] [N] = 36.00 [INPUT] [N] [N] = 36.60 (if the integer above displays as 37, instead of 36, no matter – [INPUT] [N] [N] as above).

If you knew the number of months and wished merely to find the correct number of odd days, you could, in order to save time, simply key-in the known integer value (here 36) [INPUT] [N] [INPUT] [N] [N] = the correct value for [N].

36 [INPUT] [N] [INPUT] [N] [N] = 36.60

Sometimes, with a difficult series of parameters, there can be no final solution. For instance, retain the above data, save that for $115.01 monthly payments substitute $123. Find the odd days.

In this case, the above guessing iterative process will be unproductive. Consequently, the only method is to find the *integer* value by trial and error.

33 months will provide payments of 123.19 and as this value is so near the required $123 it is unlikely that there are any odd days. This is confirmed when, using the above [INPUT] [N] method, the values displayed [LEFT] (123.19) and [RIGHT] (123.00) are sufficiently close to make further calculations obviously pointless.

Very occasionally, constant iteration may produce two values for [N]. For example, [N] might be 26.014462 or 36.433401. First discover the payments resulting from the integer values, 26 or 36 months. While the 26th month might look more attractive being, perhaps, nearer to the required payment, the odd days will be nil, for .014462 x 360/12 = .433860: whereas .466491 x 360/12 = 13.99, namely 36 months and 14 odd days.

The following programs are available on request

Leasing balances

Net calculations for annuity bonds (as instanced by the example of the Zimbabwe annuity)

Dollar semi–annual medium–term certificates of deposit (not traded on the London market)

Programs, particular to the reader's own business, can be supplied providing the requirement lends itself to the HP programming format.

<u>Contact either</u>:
Hewlett–Packard Ltd.
Calculator Support Group
King Street Lane,
Winneresh.
Wokingham.
Berks RG11 5AR
Telephone (0734) 784774

or:
Kogan Page Ltd.
Publishers
120 Pentonville Road
LONDON N1 9JN.
Telephone 01-278-0433

BTC 3 NOM% : $(-(-COST + FEE + DEP) - RV \times (SPPV (NOM\% \div P/YR : MONS))) \div (\# ADV + USPV (NOM\% \div P/YR : \# SPR)) = PMT$

↓

COST = CASH PRICE   P/YR : PAYMENTS PER YR 12m (4Q)

FEE = SELF EXPLANATORY   MONS = MONTH THAT RESIDUAL WILL BE PAID

DEP = DEPOSIT   # ADV = No OF ADV PAYMENTS

R.V = RESIDUAL VALUE   # SPR = No OF MTHS FOR AGREEMENT

NOM% = TRUE RATE   PMT = INSTALMENT AMOUNT

1.E   COST = 1000   P/YR = 12

        NOM = 17.92% (10/flat)   # SPR = 36 MTHS   = 36.11

2/   VAT DEFERRAL   1000 + 175 VAT   + 36 DEFERRED 2 MTHS

      2ND MONTH

    COST = 1175   RV = 175   NOM = 17.92   P/YR = 12   # SPR = 36

    MONS = MONTH 2

    PAYMENT = 36.30